OBAMINATION
The Misadministration
of Barack Hussein Obama

OBAMINATION
The Misadministration of Barack Hussein Obama

Thurman Leonard Smith

Smithurmann Publishing
Winchester Massachusetts
www.smithurmann.com
781-729-6844 / 800-982-0055

ISBN 978-1-7335095-0-3

Library of Congress Control Number 2018914795

The cover photo was obtained from Google Images, attributed to the BBC, which on a request for permission, replied that the photo was not theirs. Any claimant should contact the author at thurmansmith@efrllc.com.

Contents

Forward

Barack Hussein Obama was surely the most un-American president to date, at least to those of us who always thought that America was characterized by individualism, self-reliance, entrepreneurship and a shared understanding of the need for a strong national government when it comes to dealing with foreign affairs. In Contrast, the themes in his term were collectivization vs. individualism, hostility to business, disrespect for traditional social norms, weaponizing the agencies of the federal government against his foes, a tendency to act without concurrence of Congress in areas where it should have been consulted, a negative attitude towards the military and police, prevarication beyond the norm for presidents, a racial chip on his shoulder, weakness in dealing with foreign adversaries, and in foreign relations a tilt towards things Islamic.

Part One covers Obama's domestic, foreign and social policies, everything except ObamaCare, which is covered in Part Two. The topics are categorical rather than chronological, and some may slightly overlap. I use "regime" instead of "administration" as the former seems more appropriate for the dictatorial style of this president.

One object of this book is to give readers some ammunition in any discussions on the Obama years. Modern social media has heated up political argument, but thanks to the Internet one can more research more subjects more easily. Thus, the inclusion of web sources in context. The links are not essential for understanding the material, but visiting the websites will add depth.

The full URL is shown to aid a search for the content should the article have been moved to another location on the website. But **the ID before the URL -such as C1-AA- holds an imbedded link for online readers.** Do not click on the URL to the right even if it, or part of it, looks live. Print readers, or those using a reader that is not connected to the Internet, can easily access the sites on a connected device using the list of URLs (with their IDs) at www.smithurmann.com/links.htm. Here the tags are just for identification – so do click on the URL.

The links were tested at time of publication, but if any do not work, do let me know at thurmansmith@efrllc.com.

I was aided by author and political maven Michael Isenberg (*Full Asylum, The Thread of Reason* -.MonteFerropress.com) whose comments made for valuable improvements in content and organization.

Thurman Leonard Smith
Winchester, Massachusetts
December 31, 2018

Part One
All but ObamaCare

"We are five days away from fundamentally transforming the United States of America." —Barack Obama, October 30, 2008

Unfortunately when Obama set out to fundamentally transform America, he succeeded. At least in part. As harmful as the Johnson and Carter administrations were for the country, they were nothing compared with the impact of the presidency of Barack Hussein Obama. At almost every turn, he made the choice that was the least beneficial to the country's economy, security, morale and morals. First let's review his unusual background.

THURMAN LEONARD SMITH

~1~
An Unusual Background

The Constitution requires that presidents be "natural born." There is lack of agreement as to exactly what that phrase means, but the idea certainly was to better ensure that presidents were "of the land" and thus less likely to harbor, consciously or otherwise, any allegiances to other countries or ideals contrary to American ones. Given Obama's very unusual early background, the un-American nature of many of his acts as president should not be a surprise.

Of the land?

Questions of whether he was born in Hawaii or Kenya, where his mother visited her husband Barack Hussein Obama,

Sr. around that time, plagued Obama throughout his career. His avoidance of confronting questions raised about his birthplace is outlined in this article from Facts are Facts:

> C1-AA https://www.facts-are-facts.com/article/barack-obama-really-made-in-the-usa

Regardless of whether he was born inside or outside the U.S., his mother was American, and so he was a citizen at birth. What counts, however, is his early experiences and parenting, and these were surely not "of the land."

His white mother, who was raised by socialists, met his father, a socialist economist for the Kenyan government while he was on a Kenyan-government sponsored program at the University of Hawaii. When Obama was two, his father left him and his mother, and returned to Kenya. A divorce followed. Obama's mother married another foreign student at UH, Lolo Soetoro, an Indonesian Muslim. From ages six to ten Obama was raised in Indonesia by his mother and stepfather. The register at his elementary school there listed him as "Barry Soetoro' noting his religion as Muslim, the prevailing religion in that part of the country, and his citizenship as Indonesian.

For better educational opportunities, his mother sent him back to Hawaii in 1971 (at age 11), where he was cared for by his maternal grandmother. He attended the exclusive Punahou School from fifth grade to graduation.

Adding to the mystery is that his social security number is one of a series that would have been issued to a resident of Connecticut, where he never resided. The best explanation I have found for his improbable SSN is this 2012 posting by Jack Cashill in The American Thinker blog:

C1-AB http://www.american-thinker.com/articles/2012/09/a_possible_explanation_for_obamas_connecticut_social_security_number.html

Radical influences

Obama's autobiography lauds Frank Marshall Davis, as a most important mentor from age 8 to 16. Davis (1905-1987) was a Communist Party USA (CPUSA) propagandist in Chicago and Hawaii. The FBI had Davis under investigation or surveillance for 19 years, compiling a 600-page FBI file. He was on the FBI's 'Security Index A'. In 1948, the Kremlin ordered CPUSA to agitate for a U.S. withdrawal from Hawaii, as its naval forces were considered an obstacle to Soviet expansion in Asia. CPUSA assigned Frank Marshall Davis to Honolulu, where he began writing for the Communist Newspaper, the Honolulu Record in 1948. In his columns, Davis flawlessly mirrored official Soviet propaganda —he blamed American capitalism for starting World War II, denounced the Marshall Plan, preached wealth redistribution, nationalization of industry and government healthcare, while bashing Wall Street. In 1956, Davis was subpoenaed by the Senate Subcommittee on Un-American Activities and pleaded the Fifth.

While at Occidental College, Obama traveled in the same circles as former Marxist Dr. John Drew, who started what became the Democratic Socialist Alliance, then Democratic Socialists of America, in which Obama was active from time to time. In a February 2011 American Thinker article, Drew

5

described his influence on Obama in this way: "At that time [1980] the future president was a doctrinaire Marxist revolutionary, although perhaps considering conventional politics as a more practical road to socialism."

C1-AC
https://www.americanthinker.com/articles/2011/
02/meeting_young_obama.html

Obama's circle included some very anti-American radicals. Chief among them was Weather Underground terrorists Bill Ayres and Bernadine Dohrn. The Weather Underground was a self-described communist revolutionary group with the intent to "overthrow imperialism," that conducted a campaign of bombing public buildings (including police stations, the US Capitol Building, and the Pentagon) during the 1960s and 1970s in response to US involvement in the Vietnam War. Ayres' home was the location for a fund-raiser for Obama's run for the Illinois Senate. And hard-left funder George Soros held fund-raisers for Obama when he was running for the U.S. Senate.

This Western Journal article covers many of Obama's radical associations in some detail:

C1-AD https://www.westernjournal.com/just-radical-people-influenced-barack-hussein-obama/

Were leaders in the Democrat Party unaware of these associations at nomination time in 2008?

~2~
Domestic Dysfunction

Department of Misjustice

To an extent that well exceeded the John Kennedy-Robert Kennedy President-Attorney General relationship, Obama's Eric Holder was on many occasions a political enforcer doing the bidding of his boss. In 2013, after he left office, he described himself in a radio interview as "still Obama's wingman." Holder's successor, Loretta Lynch, is best known for a meeting on her plane at the Phoenix airport with Bill Clinton where, we are to believe, they talked about their grandchildren (Ms. Lynch has none) near the end of the FBI's investigation into Hillary's obvious gross negligence in handling of classified information at the State Department (or, as the FBI's James Comey referred to it, the "matter" of her "extreme carelessness.") What follows are some, just some, of the uncivic practices of these two exponents of political expediency.

Voting: worst practices

Voter intimidation in the City of Brotherly Love

At Holder's DOJ, almost every issue that could be screened through a racial angle *was* screened through a racial angle. The Obama regime began in the aftermath of the 2008 election, during which there was blatant voter intimidation by members of the New Black Panther Party in Philadelphia.

As witnessed by Bartle Bull, a former civil rights lawyer and publisher of *The Village Voice*, two Black Panthers in paramilitary garb stood at the entrance to a polling place near downtown Philadelphia. One of them brandished a nightstick and pointed it at white voters, and both made racial threats. Mr. Bull said he heard one yell "You are about to be ruled by the black man, cracker!" This video conveys the scene:

C2-AA
https://www.youtube.com/watch?v=qX4dcvlYk9A

Such abuse was ripe for investigation and prosecution, but the case was dropped by the new attorney general, despite the strong preference of the Civil Rights Commission.

This 2010 article by Hans von Spakovsky of the Heritage Foundation outlines how the DOJ avoided application of the law to this case:

C2-AB http://www.heritage.org/commentary/voter-intimidation-new-black-panther-style

One would think that, as a former law-school instructor who specialized in voting rights, a President Obama and his chief law enforcement officer would be aware of how important even-handed application of the law is to election integrity.

Attacks on state voting procedures

The Obama Justice Department consistently approached state voter registration issues from the assumption that African-Americans were being disenfranchised, even if they weren't, and discouraged state efforts to improve voter integrity.

Hostility to voter identification

Although a picture ID requirement is ubiquitous in modern life, many jurisdictions do not require one to register or vote. Eric Holder left no opportunity to restrain state efforts to improve the integrity of their voter rolls, such as by requiring a picture ID or other proof of citizenship to register or evidence identity at the polls.

To show how lax voter verification can be, Project Veritas sent an undercover journalist (white, no less) to Eric Holder's poling location in Washington, where at check-in he asked the clerk "Do you have an Eric Holder?" and was promptly offered a ballot.

> C2-AC https://www.projectveritas.com/u-s-ag-eric-holders-ballot-offered-to-total-stranger/

Section Five abuse

Section five of the Voting Rights Act of 1965 (VRA) was enacted to freeze changes in election practices or procedures in certain jurisdictions in the South until the new procedures were determined to have neither discriminatory purpose nor effect. It was enacted in 1965 as temporary legislation, to expire in five years, and applicable only to certain states, but kept getting extended by Congress and is now due to expire in 2031. The specially covered jurisdictions were identified in Section Four by a formula.

The Civil Rights Division of the Obama Justice Department abused its authority and power under this section on numerous occasions and consistently opposed efforts to verify voters at the polls. Some examples follow.

South Carolina

In 2012, the Palmetto state was forced to spend $3.5 million litigating a specious objection filed by the Division against its voter ID law. A federal court found that there was no basis for the objection.

Florida

Also, in 2012, the DOJ sent a legally dubious letter to the Sunshine state claiming that its government was violating Section Five because it had not precleared the state's removal of non-citizens who had unlawfully registered to vote (five Florida counties are covered under Section Five). This was despite the fact that non-citizens commit a felony when they register to vote. This 2014 follow-up news release by Judicial Watch explains why Florida had good reason to clean up its voter rolls:

C2-AD
https://www.judicialwatch.org/blog/2014/03/fla-tv-station-exposes-voter-fraud-doj-sues-state-to-stop-purging-rolls/

North Carolina

In 2013, the Tar Heel state implemented a number of practical election reforms designed to make it harder to commit voter fraud and reduce the costs of running elections. In 2014, the DOJ and certain civil rights groups sued the state, arguing that these changes adversely affected blacks: *(North Carolina, et al. v. North Carolina State Conference of the NAACP, et al.)*. Holder's DOJ used Section Two (race or color) of the VRA in a suit to undo these efforts, even though there was much evidence of ample voting participation by blacks. Ron Christie explains the conflict in this 2014 Daily Beast article following a loss by DOJ in a federal district court:

C2-AE https://www.thedailybeast.com/hey-eric-holder-voter-id-isnt-stuck-in-1965

The DOJ appealed to the Court of Appeals and won, so the state appealed to the Supreme Court. In 2017 the post-Scalia Court had only 8-members, and it was reluctant to take on important cases with the risk of a tie vote. So, it refused to rule, leaving the state without its reforms.

Some relief from an overbearing DOJ came in the 2013 *Shelby County v. Holder* decision, which struck down the formulas in Section Four for determining whether a voting jurisdiction still needed DOJ permission to make a change in voting procedures. This 2013 Washington Times article describes the case:

C2-AF
https://www.washingtontimes.com/news/2013/jun/2
5/court-past-voting-discrimination-no-longer-held/

Texas

In 2013, the Holder Justice Department filed a similar lawsuit against the State of Texas. In this case, the lawsuit was still active when the Trump administration took office; it dropped the government's appeals. This Washington Times article describes the suit:

C2-AG
https://www.washingtontimes.com/news/2013/aug/
22/holder-sues-texas-stop-voter-id-law/

Selective prosecution

Political considerations were clearly behind the decision to forcefully prosecute author and film-maker Dinesh D'Souza in 2014 for a straw-donor campaign-finance infraction involving very small amounts, the type of offense that is customarily settled by payment of an administrative fine to the Federal Election Commission.

D'Souza, born in India, came to the U.S. in 1978 as a Rotary Youth Exchange student in Arizona, then went on to Dartmouth College where he wrote for the conservative journal Dartmouth Review. After Dartmouth he wrote for the Heritage Foundation and was a policy adviser for the Reagan administration. He became a U.S. citizen in 1991. After writing six books taking bold positions on various public policy issues

—especially where cultural and moral issues interact with politics — he co-produced in 2012 the controversial film *2016: Obama's America,* which traced the president's politics to the Communism and anti-colonialism of his Kenyan father, and such mentors as Frank Marshall Davis. In making the film, he sought out and interviewed Obama's half-brother, who was clearly in need of medical care. D'Souza covered the costs. The trailer for the film can be found at the below link:

<u>C2-AH</u> https://www.dineshdsouza.com/films/2016-obamas-america/

Obama was enraged and had his Justice Department turn the campaign contribution case into a multiple felony indictment. D'Souza was forced to post $500,000 in bail. He did avoid prison, but the U.S. judge sentenced him to serve eight months in a halfway house ("community confinement center") after he pleaded guilty to the charges. He was still under a five-year probation imposition when Trump pardoned him in 2018.

Campaign finance irregularities ignored

The 2008 Obama campaign was caught illegally hiding nearly $2 million in ineligible contributions (in addition to dragging its feet on the return of millions more in suspect donations). It should come as no surprise that the Obama Justice Department didn't prosecute anyone. It was considered a mere hiccup: resolved by a fine, as described in this Politico article:

<u>C2-AI</u>
https://www.politico.com/story/2013/01/obama-2008-campaign-fined-375000-085784

For good reasons, it is illegal to raise funds for federal campaigns from foreign entities. So, the Obama campaign's effort to raise foreign money over the Internet via online credit card contributions was troubling. The Government Accountability Institute issued a report showing potential violations of federal election law by failing to prevent the use of fraudulent or foreign credit card transactions on the official Obama for America donation page. This 2012 TownHall article by Katie Pavlich goes into more detail:

C2-AJ https://townhall.com/tipsheet/katie-pavlich/2012/10/08/exposing-barack-obamas-illegal-foreign-campaign-money-loophole-n710300

The war on police

In a federation such as the United States, everyday policing is a function of the several states and their subdivisions (counties and municipalities), not the national government. In violation of this principle, and once again seeing everything through the racial angle, the Obama/Holder Justice Department declared war on local and state police. Their war took two forms:

Federal takeover of local police management

No opportunity was lost to, in effect, federalize some police departments, in many cases deploying an agency known as the Community Relations Service. This was a public relations unit in DOJ established in the Civil Rights Act of 1964 and augmented in 2009 after the Matthew Shepard incident and using the 1994 Violent Crime Control and Law Enforcement Act (courtesy of Rodney King).

The approach was to initiate an investigation, make an adverse finding of uneven policing, threaten a law suit, and then force local police departments into consent decrees that allow for court monitoring for several years. What was different in the Obama years from earlier uses of this procedure was the emphasis on implicit or unconscious bias. This 2015 Daily Caller article provides an overview of DOJ's agenda, especially with regard to race and gender:

C2-AK http://dailycaller.com/2015/05/28/doj-police-probes-and-consent-decrees-spike-under-obama/

The cities selected for consent decrees leading to DOJ supervision had been stressed by uncivil and sometimes violent reactions to police called in to deal with serious infractions by one or more members of the same racial cohort as the protesters. In most cases, the DOJ action did not stem from a decision by police to just go out and start harassing and arresting people in these subsets for no reason. The best known cases of these DOJ supervisions are New Orleans, Ferguson Missouri and Baltimore.

2010 New Orleans

This process started from a hurricane Katrina incident and quickly got very messy. Hearing reports of shots being fired at New Orleans police on a bridge, more police forces were called to the scene. In the melee on the bridge, police shot and killed two black males (who turned out to be unarmed); four other black civilians were wounded. Although four of the seven officers were black, civil-rights warriors tagged this incident as racial aggression by the police.

State prosecutors made charges against the police, but flubbed their case in court, leading to a mistrial. The U.S. Attorney then filed an indictment alleging civil-rights and firearm violations. He was not an honest man. Andrew McCarthy in this 2015 National Review article describes the sordid affair of an errant U.S. prosecutor who used devious methods to target New Orleans police officials and that lead to a federal takeover:

C2-AL http://www.nationalreview.com/article/422923/justice-departments-grotesque-misconduct-against-new-orleans-cops-andrew-c-mccarthy

2014 Ferguson, Missouri

Local investigators in the Michael Brown shooting heard from twenty-two individuals who said they were eyewitnesses and that they saw Brown's hands were up when was shot by officer Darren Wilson. But DOJ investigators found these accounts to be unreliable and inconsistent with physical and forensic evidence. The press spread the meme anyway, and so "hands up - don't shoot" became the rallying cry for the George Soros-backed counter-productive Black Lives Matter (BLM) movement and an excuse to supervise the Ferguson police department.

Americans value separation of powers both within the national government and among the states. Citizen influence diminishes as layers of control climb to a distant and less controllable authority. If the government is to be truly of the people, then most of everyday life that might involve government must be, at first recourse, a matter for local authority. So, the dangers of federal supervision of local police imposed on Ferguson are a serious setback for self-rule and values necessary for a functioning republic. These dangers of such top-down intervention are well described in this 2017 Federalist Society article by D.C McAllister:

> C2-AM http://thefederalist.com/2014/09/08/why-ferguson-could-lead-to-federal-takeovers-of-local-police/

2016 Baltimore

In this city with the 2nd-highest large-city murder rate (2017), a long difficult police/community relationship came to a violent head in the death of Freddie Gray, who was carelessly transported after his arrest for carrying a knife that was illegal in Baltimore. After his death, there was a decrease in police street surveillance and arrests, and an increase in killings, as police reacted to violent anti-police street protests.

In an August 2016 New York Post article, Eugene O'Donnell describes how wrong a DOJ report was that blamed public safety problems in Baltimore on the police rather than a host of larger social and political causes:

C2-AN https://nypost.com/2016/08/11/obamas-justice-dept-did-a-clueless-hit-job-on-baltimore-cops/

In many cases, municipalities that signed consent decrees saw a police paralysis that led to rising crime. The principal victims were in minority communities that suffer when law enforcement retreats. In a 2017 issue of City Journal, the Manhattan Institute's Heather Mac Donald describes how the Trump Justice Department is trying to restore the legitimacy of local policing where the Obama-era DOJ had interfered:

C2-AO https://www.city-journal.org/html/how-stifle-policing-15432.html

Denigration of local police

The other aspect of Obama's war on police was a series of comments that bad-mouthed local police forces. For example, early in his first term he inserted himself in the aftermath of a disorderly conduct arrest after the Cambridge, Massachusetts police responded to a report of what looked like two people attempting to break into a house. It was a false alarm; Harvard professor Henry Louis Gates, who is black, was just trying to open the jammed door of his own house, with the help of his driver, after returning from a trip. Obama assumed that the rough encounter was mostly due to the officer's behavior and said "the police acted stupidly" without knowing the details of the exchange.

Obama gave credibility to such groups as Black Lives Matter. Although the number of people, both black and white, shot by police in the U.S. is of concern to many well meaning individuals, BLM has only made the situation worse. It fosters notions not connected with reality regarding miscreant behavior and a necessary police response to it. An April, 2017 internal FBI report suggested that the media, politicians and BLM have turned people against the police and emboldened people not to comply with police orders. A summary of this report can be found on this FoxNews site:

C2-AP http://www.foxnews.com/us/2017/05/12/fer-guson-effect-legit-police-laud-fbi-report-that-says-cop-killings-new-norm.html

In July, 2016 black army reservist Micha Johnson killed five police officers on a detail for a Dallas BLM rally that was protesting recent police shootings of two black men in other states. During lengthy negotiations from the garage where he had fled, Johnson said he wanted to kill white people, especially white officers. William Johnson, executive director of the National Association of Police Organizations, described what he saw as the "war on cops" after the shootings:

C2-AQ
https://www.politico.com/story/2016/07/obama-war-on-cops-police-advocacy-group-225291

Purging fugitives from the background check system

Making the job of the police more difficult and dangerous was the purge by the Obama Justice Department of more than 500,000 fugitives from the federal gun background check system, as revealed in a March 2018 Senate Judiciary Committee hearing by FBI Deputy Director David Bodwich. This move made no sense and wasn't called for by any law or custom. Katie Pavlich goes into detail in this 2018 TownHall article:

C2-AR https://townhall.com/tipsheet/katie-pavlich/2018/03/16/fbi-the-obama-regime-purged-500000-fugitives-from-the-gun-background-check-system-n2461438

Ignoring criminal history for applicants for federal jobs.

In May 2016 Obama issued a new order prohibiting federal agencies from asking applicants for employment about their criminal history. The stated purpose was to make public-sector jobs more accessible to convicts recently released from prison. The verdict is still out, but this addition to an earlier Roadmap to Re-entry program might introduce dangers to co-workers for and users of federal services where additions to staff might have been unreformed ex-cons. Below is the announcement and a comment by Judicial Watch:

C2-AS
https://www.judicialwatch.org/blog/2016/05/obama-orders-fed-agencies-to-stop-asking-job-applicants-about-criminal-history/

Domestic spying and misuse of federal resources to affect an election

In America the federal government must not use its resources for political purposes. The Hatch Act limits certain political activities of most executive branch employees. FBI activities are supposed to be for investigations of possible violations of federal law, and the CIA's resources are strictly for foreign matters. But these restrictions did not get in the way of the Obama regime when it decided to get information on perceived enemies. Targets were congressional committees, reporters, and a candidate for president and later president-elect. These activities may have been part of a larger effort by the regime to manipulate the results of the 2016 presidential election.

Illegal spying on:

Reporters

In 2010 a Fox News reporter assigned to the State Department, James Rosen, was working on a story about negotiations with North Korea. Holder's Justice Department named Rosen in an affidavit as a possible co-conspirator with a South Korean-born State Department contractor. It then began to collect Rosen's telephone records and personal emails, as well as his movements to and from the State Department. Rosen claimed that his parents' phone line records were also collected. This 2013 article in The Guardian outlines the dubious process:

C2-AT
https://www.theguardian.com/world/2013/may/20/f
ox-news-reporter-targeted-us-government

In 2012 Holder's Justice Department subpoenaed telephone

records of twenty Associated Press reporters in a quest to discover how the AP learned of CIA anti-terrorist activity in Yemen. The New York Times covered the story in this 2013 video article:

C2-AU
https://www.nytimes.com/2013/05/14/us/phone-records-of-journalists-of-the-associated-press-seized-by-us.html

Former CBS Washington bureau investigative star reporter Sharyl Attkisson discovered in 2014 that her laptop had been hacked by an as-yet unknown federal entity after reporting all too truthfully about "Fast and Furious," which is discussed below. Attkisson may have been in the sights of the regime, as she had recently reported that then first lady Hillary Clinton's claim of coming under fire on a 2008 trip to Bosnia was false. Her suit against the FBI for disclosure of her FBI file is still unresolved. This blog by John Rappoport outlines her case:

C2-AV https://jonrappoport.word-press.com/2017/01/31/actual-hacking-every-re-porter-needs-to-understand-sharyl-attkissons-case-against-the-us-government/

A congressional committee

Under our Constitution, the three branches are co-equal, so one would not expect that one branch would trespass on another. But in 2014 the CIA read emails of investigators for the Senate Intelligence Committee, which was investigating the agency's detention and interrogation program in the post-911 war on terror. This episode is described in this New York Times article:

21

C2-AW
https://www.nytimes.com/2014/08/01/world/senate-
intelligence-commitee-cia-interrogation-report.html

A candidate for office

The most impeachment-worthy offense of the Obama gang
surely mst be the activities that senior officials at several departments and agencies, especially his FBI, undertook to spy on
Donald Trump during his campaign and in the pre-inauguration
period. It's a messy story one would expect in banana republics
or totalitarian dictatorships, but not in the United States of
America.

FISA follies

One way to get legal cover such activity is to persuade a Foreign Intelligence Surveillance Act (FISA) judge that an "American person" was a danger to the country from involvement with
a hostile foreign power. It seems that's what the FBI did in getting warrants -three times- to spy on Carter Page, an American
petroleum industry consultant with some activities in Russia
and briefly a foreign-policy adviser to the Trump campaign
(who never met Trump). The main evidence to persuade the
judge was a report produced for the Hillary Campaign by liber-
ally-inclined opposition research firm, Fusion GPS, and that
was written by a British ex-spy who gathered uncorroborated
scurrilous tales from his former Russian contacts (or maybe just
created) about Trump's behavior while in Moscow arranging
the 2013 Miss Universe pageant. It is curious that the fees to
Fusion GPS were paid via the Clinton campaign's law firm, no
doubt to disguise the indirect foreign contribution to the effort.

(As of this writing Carter Page has yet to be charged with a crime, but in October 2018 sued the Democrat National Committee and their law firm for defamation.)

It is the abuse of the using a FISA warrant that is the heart of all the hostile forces rallied against Trump during the late Obama period. One of the best descriptions of what happened, and what was so wrong, is this 2017 National Review article by Andrew McCarthy, who served as an Assistant United States Attorney for the Southern District of New York in the Clinton years:

C2-AX
https://www.nationalreview.com/2017/05/nsa-illegal-surveillance-americans-obama-administra-tion-abuse-fisa-court-response/

The FBI gets political

In the below 2018 update, McCarthy describes how the texts between two high-level FBI officials reveal the real motives for the Russian-collusion investigation was to deflect attention and resources from the Hillary email investigation by drawing attention to Trump:

C2-AY
https://www.nationalreview.com/2018/05/strzok-page-texts-trump-russia-investigation-origins/

The Epoch Times has produced an informative chart outlining the surveillance activities and the various parties involved:

C2-AZ
https://www.theepochtimes.com/assets/uploads/2018/03/15/FISA_SPYING_INFOGRAPHIC.jpg

In May 2018, the New York Times revealed a leak from the Mueller investigation that U.S. intelligence resources did spy on the Trump campaign and even had a plant within the campaign. It was Cambridge University professor Stefan Halper, who had high-level gigs with both U.S. and British intelligence. He also had credibility within Republican circles as a long-time CIA asset who worked for the Nixon, Ford and Reagan administrations. Curiously, from July 2016 to September 2017 he was paid $400,000 from a Defense Department account, but wasn't working on a DOD project.

This Federalist Society article by Mollie Hemingway summarizes the takeaways, the largest of which is that we had a government that thought it was OK to use the powers of its law enforcement and intelligence agencies to surveil and target Americans based on their political views and affiliations:

> C2-BA http://thefederalist.com/2018/05/17/10-key-takeaways-from-new-york-times-error-ridden-defense-of-fbi-spying-on-trump-campaign/

Unmasking Trump persons

Section 702 of the Foreign Surveillance Act requires that names of Americans heard in intercepts are supposed to be masked. In early 2017, the House Intelligence Committee investigating alleged collusion between the Trump campaign and Russia uncovered the apparent deliberate unmasking of "U.S. persons" connected with the Trump campaign in intelligence intercepts. Two culprits have been identified: One was Obama's national security adviser Susan Rice; the other was Obama's U.N. ambassador Samantha Power.

David French, in this September 2017 National Review article, describes the apparent motivation behind this highly irregular activity, particularly by former national security adviser Susan Rice:

C2-BB
https://www.nationalreview.com/2017/09/susan-rice-devin-nunes-unmasking-controversy-did-rice-lie/

In October 2017, Judicial Watch filed a Freedom of Information Act (FOIA) request for documents related to Samantha Power's unmasking activities. State refused to honor the request, so JW later initiated a FOIA lawsuit against the State Department for the documents:

C2-BC https://www.judicialwatch.org/press-room/press-releases/judicial-watch-sues-state-department-samantha-powers-unmasking-documents/

Actions to discourage prosecution of Hillary Clinton

The carefully contrived and highly irregular actions by Obama's FBI director James Comey to pre-empt Justice from bringing charges on the laws Hillary broke regarding mishandling of classified information must certainly be regarded as severely contrary to the public interest. The law and State Department policy requires that official electronic correspondence be made through secure government servers, for a host of reasons, not the least of which is containment of classified information.

Instead of following standard practice, Hillary had a private server installed in the basement of the Clinton residence in Chappaqua, New York and created an email account (hdr22@clintonemail.com) which she used to send both personal and official emails. Also, she forwarded State emails to her assistant Huma Abedin, which also ended up on Huma's husband Anthony Weiner's laptop (along with evidence of his "sexting" with a minor female teenager). Given the very insecure server setup, it would not be surprising to learn someday that foreign interests had intercepted communications on it.

The FBI's investigation was tilted to go easy on Hillary. Her lawyers were allowed to delete 30,000 emails that they (not FBI investigators) deemed personal. In his July, 2016 press conference, Comey reported that from the group of 30,000 emails returned to the State Department and recovered from archives and her correspondents' systems, 113 emails were determined to contain classified information at the time they were sent or received and 2,000 additional emails were "up-classified" later to make them Confidential. Limiting the scope of the FBI investigation was the admitted destruction of some of Hillary's mobile devices by her staff.

Despite these serious infractions of federal law regarding handling of secrets, Comey chose not to prosecute the former Secretary of State. His decision was likely closely tied to the deepstate effort to spy on and undermine candidate and president-elect Trump. A complete timeline on Obama-era domestic spying from April 2009 to October 2017 by investigative reporter Sharyl Attkisson is available on her website:

C2-BD https://sharylattkisson.com/2017/12/05/obama-era-surveillance-timeline/

Other domestic divergences from good government

Pandering pardons

Obama mostly commuted sentences rather than granted out-right pardons. And most of those commutations were for excessively long sentences for low-level drug crimes. Wise or not, his commutations totaled 1,715, far more than by any other president. But Obama wasn't above pandering to Democrat voting blocks in two last-hour clemency actions.

A Puerto-Rican Terrorist

Puerto Rican terrorist Oscar Lopez Rivera got a pardon. He was a leader in the Armed Forces of National Liberation, or FALN, which conducted a nine-year campaign of terror throughout the United States. Their best known assault was a 1975 bombing in historic Fraunces Tavern in New York, which killed four people and injured sixty, many of whom were maimed. FALN wanted to establish a Marxist republic in Puerto Rico. Lopez, a community organizer in Chicago, joined the FALN in 1974. He recruited and trained a small army of terrorists to murder his fellow Americans and built bomb factories. He taught the young and impressionable how to make devices that would kill and maim. He was a fugitive for five years before his arrest in 1981, when police discovered six pounds of dynamite in his Chicago apartment. In his trial, he admitted to doing all he had been accused of and showed no remorse. Thanks to Obama he's out and about, perhaps to plan more terror.

An Army deserter

Bradley Manning got a commutation. This leaker of military and diplomatic secrets in the Afghanistan arena could have been tried for treason, given he was in a war zone and placed the lives of Americans and allies in danger, but was instead given a 35-year sentence for multiple counts including violations of the Espionage Act and copying and disseminating classified military field reports, State Department cables, and assessments of detainees held at Guantanamo. He served seven years and cost taxpayers even more than usual in such cases by convincing a gullible command to accommodate his delusion that he was female.

Politicizing the Internal Revenue Service

There are a host of organizations that are formed to promote a cause or change in public policy, not to make money. Those that are genuine charities seek a 501(c)(3) designation, which makes contributions tax deductible. Others make no claim to be a charity, but apply to IRS to be considered a "social welfare" 501(c)(4) non-profit, contributions to which are not deductible. They may conduct unlimited lobbying but political activity is supposed to be secondary.

Prior to the 2012 election, it became evident that the IRS was delaying action on applications for organizations with an apparent purpose opposite of the policy preferences of the Obama regime. Especially delayed were those with names that included terms like "Tea Party" or that indicated a conservative stance. Liberal groups also complained of delays, but in 2013 a House Oversight Committee and the Treasury Inspector General concluded that the IRS was applying excessive scrutiny mostly to conservative groups. The Obama Justice Department abjured from filing any charges.

In response to these delays, more than 400 conservative groups affected by the IRS stance on their applications sued the IRS. In the fall of 2017, the Trump regime agreed to settle two of the largest lawsuits, with payments, an acknowledgment of wrongdoing and an apology for the previous administration's malfeasance. This 2017 Washington Times article is a good review of this saga:

C2-BE
https://www.washingtontimes.com/news/2017/oct/2
5/trump-apologizes-irs-tea-party-targeting-faults-lo/

Conservative groups were not the only targets. Given the anti-Israel bias of the Obama regime, it was not surprising that the IRS took seven years to approve 501(c)(3) status to Z Street, which sought to educate Americans about the Middle East and Israel's defenses against terrorism.

Student loan takeover

The federal government had been involved, indirectly, in loans for higher education since 1965 (the Federal Family Education Loan program or FFEL), as a subsidizer and guarantor of loans made by banks and other private lenders, rather than as a lender itself. Initially such loans were targeted to non-credit worthy, low-income students, but later expanded to every American. Over time the FFEL program subsidies were reduced as Congress created and expanded Pell grants and other programs that targeted the less fortunate. Democrats were never keen on FFEL as they didn't like subsidies for private lenders.

The 2008 financial crisis ended lender interest in FFEL loans, so Congress passed a short-term fix. But in 2010 Obama succeeded in ending FFEL with an amendment to ObamaCare (together abbreviated as HCERA) which requires all new student loans to be made by direct government lending and increased Pell grants. A key point made by its backers was that the government would save billions and collect interest income.

Alas, what we got was a disaster. The government became a lender, but exercised hardly any of the evaluation of the credit worthiness of the borrowers that a private lender would perform. With loans so easy to get, too many Americans borrowed too much money to attend institutions that charge too much in tuition in exchange for an education of dubious professional and intellectual value. At the same time, the implicit aid encouraged colleges to increase tuition.

Preston Cooper, an analyst tracking the economics of higher education, describes below how the financial picture looked six years after HCERA. Among other observations, he estimated that the federal student loan program will come with a $170 billion price tag by 2026:

C2-BF
https://www.forbes.com/sites/prestoncooper2/2016/04/10/federal-student-loans-will-cost-taxpayers-170-billion

At the end of the third quarter of 2017, the default totaled $84 billion and the number of loans behind in payments was 4.6 million, per Education Department data. Also, the number of loans without a payment in at least a year grew to nearly 274,000. This 2017 Forbes article summarizes the ED data:

Furthermore, control of student loans gave the government unprecedented and damaging control over institutions of higher learning, as we shall see in the section on vocational schools below.

Interference in secondary education

Nowhere in the Constitution does it give the federal government any powers in the area of education. And there is good reason to keep direction and control of any public educational activities closest to the parents whose kids are in the schools.

But every so often we have a president who wants to use the federal fisc or influence to nudge secondary education to supposedly higher or more specific standards. Such guidance from the top started in Republican administrations. Ronald Reagan's education secretary William Bennett (who had promised to shutdown the Education Department) ordered the Department to create elementary and secondary education curriculum guides. George H.W. Bush's education secretary Lamar Alexander came up with his "America 2000" plan (which was not implemented). George W. Bush launched "No Child Left Behind," which was based on the erroneous assumption that the only reason for poor educational attainment was inadequate teaching, and which was criticized for teaching to the test.

With Obama, the drift to federal involvement went bigtime and it's called the Common Core State Standard (CCSS) initiative, which came out of his "Race to the Top." program. Its development is complicated, but the net result is that a small collection of persons from private groups, funded mostly by the Bill and Melinda Gates Foundation, selected, for reasons other than teaching, related educational experience or pertinent academic backgrounds, met in closed meetings and wrote the standards. To boot, no records of the proceedings were provided. Further, the members of the validation committees were generally as unqualified as the developers, and the resulting standards were not internationally benchmarked.

After several years it became obvious that CCSS's soft standards have led to poorer educational results. A 2017 article in The Hill by Jane Robbins and Emmett McGroarty outlines the many areas where educational attainment in states adopting the CCSS program has deteriorated:

C2-BH https://thehill.com/opinion/education/383464-education-report-card-shows-common-core-still-failing-us-students

Some have discerned a left-leaning, atheistic agenda in the program, such as inclusion of global warming dangers, pro-homosexual material, and the teaching of Islam. Some detail in that regard, and examples of poor and confusing pedagogics, can be found in this Conservapedia article:

C2-BI
https://www.conservapedia.com/Common_Core
astute analysis of Common Core comes from the
Massachusetts based Pioneer Institute. The Commonwealth had its own high standards and the Institute has made a case that the state's 2010
adoption of Common Core meant lower standards
and poorer achievement in math and reading
scores. Surely a $250 million Race-to-the-Top
promise if CCSS were adopted was a factor. The
below Pioneer site provides a fulsome picture of
why Common Core should be un-adopted by the
states that fell for it.

C2-BJ https://pioneerinstitute.org/common-core/

Just for laughs, view this video of how CCSS makes complicated what is a simple subtraction problem:

C2-BK
https://www.youtube.com/watch?v=2YMbKh9a0Sk

What is disturbing is that the young mother explaining the new
approach that she just learned from a talk at her local library,
doesn't seem to care that the new process is much more time
consuming than the traditional way and inappropriately abstract
for elementary school students.

Attack on vocational schools

Also, to note in the education arena is Obama's assault on for-
profit schools, ending may useful vocational programs. The
2016 assault by the Obama Education Department on the ITT
Technical Institute was a genuine loss to its current and future
students. Obama's ED forced ITT to decide to close by issuing

an un-meetable requirement for collateral with the feds to cover potential student loan defaults. The result was the stranding of 40,000 students attending 130 schools, and the discharge of 8,000 instructors. Thomas Lifson in American Thinker explains the tyrannical nature of this ukase:

C2-BL
https://www.americanthinker.com/blog/2016/09/ob
ama_administration_kills_itt_tech_strand-
ing_40000_students_and_destroy-
ing_8000_jobs.html

The PROMISE: downplaying youth criminal activity

Disparity in the incidence of youthful offenses among ethnic groups is a fact that Obama could not accept. So he established a program that kept young, non-violent misdemeanor offenders from doing any time. Called "Preventing Recidivism through Opportunities, Mentoring, Intervention, Support, and Education" (PROMISE), the program encouraged, with federal money, local law enforcement not to proceed with charges against students for such offenses as alcohol-related incidents, assault without weapon, threat, bullying, disruption on campus, drug use or possession, drug paraphernalia possession, false accusation against school staff, fighting, mutual combat, harassment, thefts, trespassing, vandalism and damage to property, and battery without serious bodily harm.

The idea was to slow the "school-to-prison pipeline." Aside from the absence of the benefit to the offenders of having to accept the consequences of their actions, this hands-off treatment often meant that their offenses were not on their record.

One deadly consequence of PROMISE was the 2018 school shooting in Parkland, Florida in which seventeen students and staff members were killed by former student Nikolas Cruz. His disciplinary history along with other details that emerged after the shooting showed law enforcement had repeatedly been warned of his violent thoughts and behaviors. In 2016 he had gotten into a fight and was suspended. In January 2017, Cruz assaulted someone and received a one-day internal suspension. He had also brought bullets and knives to school.

So Cruz would have had a record based on his earlier behavior, were it not for PROMISE. With a record, he would not have been able to buy the rifle he used in the shooting. The sorry story is explained well in this article by Ryan Nicol in the Sunshine State News:

C2-BM http://sunshinestatenews.com/story/does-broward-schools-program-coddle-troubled-students-and-excuse-dangerous-misbehavior

It is especially ironic that PROMISE was first developed by the Broward County school superintendent Robert Runcie, who was from Chicago and close to Obama's education secretary Arne Duncan, who liked the idea and furthered it nationally.

Anti-growth policies take their toll

When government policies impede the normal American exuberance, they invariably depress the economic growth that would otherwise naturally occur in an environment of freedom and opportunity, secured through limited, representative government and rule of law.

Obama's policies were a substantial departure from the post-war norm. Federal spending spiraled for many reasons: An 831-billion-dollars spending stimulus at the outset of his first term (that stimulated mostly the federal deficit), increases in transfer payments such as Social Security Disability, SNAP benefits (food-stamps), expansion of Medicare and Medicaid, ObamaCare startup costs, incentive-dampening increases in marginal tax rates, suspension of work requirements for welfare, and a slew of executive regulatory orders surely had an negative effect on growth. Also depressive was the uncertainly of business leaders about how unknown future regulations might scramble their plans for new ventures or expansion.

While there was a continuing recession into the first six months of his presidency, the weak recovery meant that in Obama's eight years, economic growth averaged an abysmally low 1.47%. By comparison the average throughout all the post-war booms and busts before 2009 was 3.4%.

Between 2009 and 2014 median household incomes stagnated and poverty increased as the expansion of welfare programs reduced the incentive to work. More than 1.5 million workers were added to the disability rolls.

The unemployment rate most commonly reported (U-3) tracks people who are looking for employment. A more revealing figure of the economic health of the nation is the full unemployment rate (U-6), which includes worker-age persons discouraged from actively seeking employment. During Obama's term U-6 rose to an unprecedented 17.1% by May 2010, and took a long time to decline to a more normal 9.4%. This MacroTrends chart shows U-6 from inception in 1994 to current:

C2-BN http://www.macrotrends.net/1377/u6-unem-ployment-rate

This analysis of the tepid Obama recovery by Americans for Prosperity compares it with that of the Reagan era:

C2-BO https://americansforprosperity.org/2-gdp-growth-not-new-normal/

Fossil Fuels Folly

Pipelines are among the safest modes of transporting hazardous materials across long distances and the rules regarding construction are clearly mandated through regulations. In 2009 TransCanada proposed a routine infrastructure project, the Keystone XL pipeline to build a more direct and larger capacity pipeline from Alberta to the Steele City, Nebraska. locus on their previously built pipeline. The new pipeline would also transport some U.S. production from Montana and North.Dakota. Obama punted approval over to State, which gave its OK in early 2015. But, ever eager to appease his climate-change crowd, Obama turned down the application. in November 2015. The oil and gas will still get to where it is needed, but by rejecting the creation of a state-of-the-art pipeline, the Obama administration forced suppliers to use less safe technology such as tanker trucks or rail.

Regulatory overkill

The Obama regime loved to regulate. His Environmental Protection Agency jammed through an average of 565 new regulations each year of his term. Over its eight years, federal agencies entered substantially more regulations in the Federal Register than any previous administration. This 2016 Daily Signal article by James Guttusa and Diane Katz surveys the scope:

C2-BP http://dailysignal.com/2016/05/23/20642-new-regulations-added-in-the-obama-presidency/

The Competitive Enterprise Institute each year publishes Ten Thousand Commandments, a report on the scope and cost of federal regulations for the previous years. Its 2017 report can be found at

C2-BQ https://cei.org/10kc2017

Perhaps the most adverse regulations in the Obama era stemmed from the augmentation of Corporate Average Fuel Economy (CAFE) standards for automobile producers. The greater chance of death and injury to persons in light vehicles involved in crashes is well known. But in 2012 Obama promulgated an outsized 54.5 miles-per-gallon standard by 2025. If that requirement had not been moderated by the Trump EPA to a more realistic 35 mpg, even lighter and more dangerous cars on the road might have been the result.

Slush funds for favored causes

With so many regulations it's not hard to run afoul of one or more. Violating regulations usually invites a legal proceeding and all too often in the Obama regime the resolution was a settlement where the fines were directed to a group whose objectives paralleled those of the president and his party. Organizations benefiting from these slush funds included the National Council of La Raza, National Urban League, and the National Community Reinvestment Coalition.

Jessica Karmasek of Legal Newsline describes what House Judiciary Chairman Bob Goodlatte (R-VA) found out about the Obama Justice Department steering of settlements to groups favored by the regime:

C2-BR
https://www.forbes.com/sites/legalnewsline/2017/1
0/24/a-smoking-gun-internal-docs-reveal-obama-
dojs-slush-fund-judiciary-chair-says

This development is especially galling given the simultaneously slow economic growth.

Weaponizing shutdowns

Disagreements over budgets and spending sometimes lead to so-called government shutdowns. These may be mostly opportunities for drama than genuine ending of vital services. Tax payments still pour in and all debt coming due must be paid first, as the Constitution makes clear that the debt of the United States "shall not be questioned." But in 2013 Obama made a shutdown worse than it had to be. For one, his regime did not encourage agencies to use carry-forward funds that they were sitting on. Nor did they encourage agencies to use transfer authority to move unused funds to other units within their department. Also, high profile national monuments and parks were barricaded so that TV cameras could show World War II veterans being turned away from the new Memorial to that conflict. But a week later, thousands of people pushing for a new immigration law were cleared by the government to proceed with a concert and rally on the Mall. The march, dubbed the "Camino Americano" was hosted by groups including the Service Employees International Union and Casa de Maryland. You can see here which groups Obama preferred.

Anti-business NRLB appointments

It was no surprise that Obama's appointments to the National Labor Relations Board would be staunchly pro-union, but he overplayed his hand in 2012 when he appointed three members as recess appointees when the Senate was not technically in recess. (The Constitution allows for appointments when the Senate is in recess). A suit by a bottling company in Washington State against these appointments was successfully argued in the Supreme Court, as described in this Washington Post Article:

C2-BS
https://www.forbes.com/sites/theemploymentbeat/20
14/06/26/obamas-nlrb-recess-appointments-
deemed-unconstitutional-100-decisions-impacted/

The Obama Board made several anti-business decisions per his union-friendly appointees. Fortunately, some of them have been overturned by the more management-sensitive Trump Board, as described in this Hinckley Allen report:

C2-BT
https://www.hinckleyallen.com/publications/republic
an-controlled-nlrb-reverses-obama-era-rulings/

Land grabs

It is said that the original thirteen states created the federal government and the federal government created the rest. Perhaps this is why the feds still own so much land in the western states. The best known case of conflict over land usage was the 2014 armed confrontation between supporters of cattle rancher

Cliven Bundy and federal law enforcement following a twenty-one-year dispute with the Bureau of Land Management over grazing fees. Bundy's ranch was in Nevada, the state with the largest (85%) share of its land is under federal control. Second in the contiguous states is Utah, which forfeits 57% to Uncle Sam. It is Utah where Obama took the most liberties to designate certain federal lands as protected monuments, using the 1906 Antiquities Act designed to protect Native American artifacts. Over his eight years, Obama created 29 national monuments, more than any other president.

The concerns of leaders in Nevada and Utah about the consequences of removing so much land from potential economic development, energy resources and other non-destructive multi-use activities is well expressed in this Newsmax commentary by Matt Anderson of the Sutherland Institute's Coalition for Self-Government following Obama's 2016 Bears Ears (Utah) and Gold Butte (Nevada) monument declarations:

C2-BU https://www.newsmax.com/thewire/jason-chaffetz-obama-midnight-monu-ment/2016/12/29/id/766012/

In 2017 President Trump substantially trimmed the scope of these monuments.

Forfeit of control of Internet names and addresses

The Internet was originally launched as a project of the U.S. Defense Department's Advanced Research Projects Agency in the 1960s. In the 1980s access to ARPANET was expanded courtesy of U.S. taxpayer-funded grants via the National

Science Foundation, and, eventually, the Internet as we know it was developed. So U.S. taxpayers paid for the creation, development and maintenance of the Internet. It is, in a very real sense, an American property.

But in 2016, the Obama regime ended the U.S. Government contract with the Internet Corporation for Assigned Names and Numbers (ICANN) even though there would be the risk of doing irreparable harm to the open Internet. The worst outcome would be censorship abroad that could lead to censorship in the United States. This has not yet happened, but why take the risk?

Attempt at "net neutrality"

The phrase sounds nice, but it could have meant less freedom for providers and users had not Trump in 2018 ended its imposition by Obama's FCC in 2016. Net neutrality means requiring all Internet Service Providers (ISPs) to treat all data on the Internet equally. They must neither favor nor discriminate against certain services, content, or applications. An ISP cannot charge additional fees for access to certain internet services, such as video streaming, even though such services place high demands on the ISP's capacity.

To ensure that each Internet Service Provider on the "Net" conformed to whatever rules the FCC might develop, the Internet would be subject to utility-type regulation. That might mean the government could insist that it needs to install its own hardware and software at critical points to monitor Internet traffic. If we value free speech, we must have privacy, but guarding the privacy of its citizens is not a strong attribute of the federal government. Further, for the Internet to continue offer increased services from imaginative providers, they must be free to be able to plan on having an open non-regulated platform. Digital marketing specialist Josh Steimle makes the argument against net neutrality in this 2014 Forbes article:

C2-BV
https://www.forbes.com/sites/joshsteimle/2014/05/
14/am-i-the-only-techie-against-net-neutrality/

Dumbing down air traffic control

In 2013 Obama implemented a plan to "transform the Federal Aviation Administration into a more diverse and inclusive workplace." The FAA based its decision on a 2013 report claiming women and minorities were under-represented among those successfully completing the Centralized Hiring Process for Air Traffic Control Specialists.

To implement the softening of standards, the FAA notified thousands of applicants to become air traffic controllers their Air Traffic Selection and Training (AT-SAT) scores were no longer valid, and they instead would have to pass a "biographical questionnaire" before being allowed to re-apply. The questionnaire awarded more points to applicants less qualified than the ones the FAA used to tap for hiring, including awarding more points to individuals with a lower aptitude in science or who had been unemployed for the previous three years.

The Mountain States Legal Foundation filed suit in 2015 on behalf of some 2,000 air traffic controller applicants who had their AT-SAT scores invalidated by the Obama regime's diversity policies. This suit was dismissed in 2016 but reactivated in 2018. In the meanwhile, airline passengers might be justified in being less sure about their safety than they were before.

Fox News anchor Tucker Carlson aired multiple segments on his show about the Obama FAA's prioritizing "diversity ahead of airline safety:"

C2-BW http://www.foxnews.com/politics/2018/06/02/obama-era-faa-hiring-rules-place-diversity-ahead-airline-safety-attorney-tells-tucker-carlson.html

For further reading

Injustice by Christian Adams; 2011, Regnery

Obama's Enforcer by John Fund and former Justice Department official Hans von Spakovsky; 2014, Broadside Books. This National Review article was adapted from the book:

C2-BX
https://www.nationalreview.com/2014/06/obamas-enforcer-john-fund-hans-von-spakovsky/

License to Lie: Exposing Corruption in the Department of Justice by Sidney Power; 2014, Brown Books.

The War on Cops by Heather Mac Donald; 2016, Encounter Books

Liars, Leakers and Liberals: The Case Against the Anti-Trump Conspiracy by Jaeanine Pirro; 2018, Center Street

The Russia Hoax: The Illicit Scheme to Clear Hillary Clinton

and Frame Donald Trump by Gregg Jarrett; 2018, Broadside Books

Spygate: The Attempted Sabotage of Donald J. Trump by Dan Bongino and D.C. McAllister; 2018

> C2-BY https://www.bongino.com/tag/spygate/

The Deep State: How an Army of Bureaucrats Protected Barack Obama and Is Working to Destroy the Trump Agenda by Jason Chaffetz; 2018, Harper Collins

This *Investor's Business Daily* Russia-Trump site is updated as needed:

> C2-BZ http://www.investors.com/russia

Scandal: How Barack Obama and Lois Lerner used the IRS to illegally target and harass Tea Party and other conservative organizations by Daniel Alman; 2017, on Kindle at

> C2-CA https://www.amazon.com/IRS-Scandal-illegally-conservative-organizations-ebook/dp/B075VXCFW6

The Student Loan Mess: How Good Intentions Created a Trillion-Dollar Problem by Joel Best and Eric Best; 2014, University of California Press

Drilling Through the Core; 2015, The Pioneer Institute:

> C2-CB https://pioneerinstitute.org/drilling-through-the-core/

~3~
External Affairs

Some observers have called Obama the first post-American president, suggesting that he believed that the U.S. was no longer the top dog. But Obama went way beyond that. He was the first president to out-wardly show contempt for the country and its unparal-leled accomplishments in establishing and preserving liberty and fostering an environment for wealth creation at home and generosity abroad.

The apology tours

It didn't take long for Obama to start diminishing America and thus weaken its power on the world stage. In office only two-and-a-half months, he set out to Strasbourg, France where he told his listeners that America has too often shown arrogance when it should have been celebrating the European Union. And further, that he was going to close the detention center in Guan-tanamo Bay because the U. S. doesn't torture its prisoners.

Although Obama never explicitly apologized on behalf of the

United States, the apologies implicit in his constant criticism of America's past caused these speeches to become known as the "Apology Tours." In the first five months of his first term, Obama can be noted for ten such apologies, as described in this June 2009 Heritage Foundation article:

C3-AA
https://www.heritage.org/europe/report/barack-obamas-top-10-apologies-how-the-president-has-humiliated-superpower

One of the last such tours was in Hiroshima, Japan in 2016. Former UN ambassador and later Trump national security adviser John Bolton analyzes this and some earlier Obama apologies in Saudi Arabia, Cuba and Russia in this 2016 New York Post article:

C3-AB https://nypost.com/2016/05/26/obamas-shameful-apology-tour-lands-in-hiroshima/

Also disturbing was Obama's habit of bowing to foreign heads of states, which is what he appeared do to King Abdullah of Saudi Arabia (2009), to the Emperor of Japan (2009), to Chinese President Hu Jainta (2010), and to Raul Castro (2013). This practice is not required by protocol, but was likely another manifestation of apologizing for the country he was representing.

Defense deprecation

Abandoning missile defenses

Another early action of the new regime was to cancel some of the most important missile defense programs that were started after the U. S. withdrew from the Anti-Ballistic Missile Treaty in 2002. The George W. Bush administration had planned with Poland and the Czech Republic for a defensive missile system to counteract increasing potential threats from Iran.

This early action was a preview of two terms of avoiding the need to improve defenses against ballistic missile and electromagnetic pulse (EMP) attacks in a period in which capabilities for this type of threat from our adversaries were rapidly increasing, especially from North Korea, China, Russia and possibly Iran. (EMP is a short burst of electromagnetic energy that can damage electronic equipment or transmissions of electricity or radio waves used for communication.)

Given the possibility of such an EMP attack, it was not wise for Obama in 2009 to have discontinued the Long-Range Navigation (LORAN-C) system of radio ship navigation assistance, which could serve as a fallback. This blog on military subjects posted a comment in 2009 on the case for keeping LORAN:

C3-AC http://www.navlog.org/obama_loran.html

A thorough analysis of the deficiencies in missile defense and military preparedness during the Obama years and suggested steps for recovery can found in a 2016 article by Michaela Dodge at the Heritage Foundation:

C3-AD
https://www.heritage.org/defense/report/president-obamas-missile-defense-policy-misguided-legacy

Diminishing military capacity and skilled officers

Obama seemed determined to weaken American military

power. An example is his 2013 order to remove nuclear-tipped Tomahawk tactical missiles from the submarine fleet. An argument for restoring these weapons was made in this 2017 article in Naval Institute Proceedings:

C3-AE
https://www.usni.org/magazines/proceedings/2017-05/bring-back-nuclear-tomahawks

Obama also cashiered many capable senior military leaders who might have a different view of the role of the military. Among them was General Carter Ham, who was relieved of his U.S. Africa Command because he disagreed with orders not to mount a rescue mission in response to the September 2012 attack in Benghazi. Over his forty years in the Army, Ham, who rose from enlisted ranks, was presented the Distinguished Service Medal and six other awards.

Also dismissed was director of the Defense Intelligence Agency, Michael Flynn, whose warnings about Al-Qaeda and other threats conflicted with Obama's preference for diplomacy. Lt. General Flynn had served in the Army for thirty-three years. In his Army career he became a specialist in defense intelligence matters, and played a key role in shaping U.S. counterterrorism strategy and dismantling insurgent networks in Afghanistan and Iraq.

This 2016 article by John Sobieski in American Thinker is a good survey of Obama's trimming of military leaders:

C3-AF
https://www.americanthinker.com/blog/2016/09/ob ama_purged_military_of_those_who_sought_victory.html

Finally, how did members of the military view the Obama era? A 2017 survey in the Military Times shows much disappointment:

C3-AG
https://www.militarytimes.com/news/2017/01/08/the-obama-era-is-over-here-s-how-the-military-rates-his-legacy/

Over half responded as either somewhat or very unfavorable. Reduction of funding and personnel were the two major concerns.

Ending the space shuttle

While the space shuttle was not a military program, there are beneficial overlaps. Starting with the cancellation of the Constellation program in 2010, Obama worked hard to diminish NASA while devoting some of its resources to promote the climate change agenda, and, yes, make Muslims feel good about their historic contribution to science, math, and engineering, as he directed his 2009 NASA director appointee Charles Bolden. Yes, in the middle ages Muslims did make many contributions to math and science, but what that has to do with NASA's 21st century mission was unclear. With the shuttle cancellation, the U.S. became dependent on Russia for conveyance of U.S. personnel to space stations. The sorry tale of the U.S. and space during the Obama years is fully outlined in this 2016 article by the staff at Capital Research Center:

C3-AH https://capitalresearch.org/article/nasa/

Disorder at the border

Encouragement of illegal immigration

Effective enforcement of immigration law has been a short-coming of all recent administrations, starting with Carter, and was particularly bad in the George W. Bush period. Some or most of such deficiencies have been characterized by insufficient enforcement, but with the Obama regime we have both a purposeful avoidance of enforcement and what seems like a planned strategy to bring in persons not of the character or number legislated by Congress (perhaps to increase the number of future Democrat voters to make up for alienated traditional constituencies?).

Below is a rough timeline of the early stages of Obama's malfeasance and neglect with regard to immigration matters.

In 2009 the themes were dismantling enforcement and pushing the idea of amnesty. A special target was the E-Verify employment eligibility program. Homeland Security secretary Janet Napolitano led the charge, surely at the direction of the new president.

In 2010 the major theme was dismantling of state and local cooperation with federal immigration enforcement, despite provisions in federal law [287(g)] outlining how state and local governments can cooperate. Especially in Obama's sights was Arizona, which in 2010 had passed laws equivalent and complementary to national immigration laws to deal with substantial illegal immigration into this border state and associated drug trafficking. In no way did the law contradict U.S. immigration law, but was seen by the state as necessary since the feds were not enforcing federal laws strongly enough. The Obama regime sued the state to wrestle back control over the issue.

The battle against Arizona was notable for a nonsensical opposition to a valid local concern of a border state. The inadequate border enforcement got so bad that a union that represents more than 7,000 detention and removal agents within Immigration and Customs Enforcement (ICE) unanimously cast a "Vote of No-Confidence" in ICE management. Nonetheless, Obama named a sanctuary city police chief as head of 287(g) programs. Later there was a reduction in detaining and deporting illegal and a sub-Rose amnesty program.

In 2011 it became evident to the relevant House committee that less than half of the southern border and only 69 of roughly 4,000 miles along the northern border was under operational control as a result of President Obama's failure to enforce U.S. immigration law.

Without a change in the law, Obama formulated a new policy in 2012 —Deferred Action for Childhood Arrivals (DACCA)— that allowed certain young persons without legal status to apply for a two-year deferral of removal proceedings and, later, to apply for work permits where there were no felonies on their records. So a new and large cohort was now competing for jobs with citizens and legal residents. Such a major change in public policy without a change in the law was worthy of impeachment.

In 2014 Obama attempted to extend DACCA privileges to additional illegal aliens, but was successfully opposed by a group of states in court. The indulgent DACCA policy was not directed to such persons arriving at the time of the policy change, but it must have given children and their families wishing to enter the U.S. the idea that they could try.

The above observations are just the some of the unwise actions in an eight-year display of dereliction of duty with regard to border control and enforcement of immigration law. A full timeline can be found in a February 2016 report by The Federation for American Immigration Reform, a leading public policy group advocating for full enforcement of existing immigration laws:

C3-AI https://fairus.org/issue/publications-resources/president-obamas-record-dismantling-immigration-enforcement

Just come on in!

Perhaps the most blatant immigration abuse by this regime was the seeming encouragement of a caravan of unaccompanied minors from Central America to cross the southern border in 2014. This invasion was surely encouraged by Obama's 2012 DACCA dictate. The response of the immigration and border control forces at hand was largely to bus them to various areas. In Marietta, California citizen protests forced back Homeland Security busses carrying immigrant children to the inland USBC processing station there. Arizona governor Jane Brewer complained to Congress that some immigrants caught at the southwest Texas border were being dropped off at bus stations in Phoenix. John Haywire of Human Events describes the scheme:

C3-AJ http://humanevents.com/2014/07/01/obamas-illegal-immigration-invitation/

In 2014 The Heritage Foundation proposed that Congress correct problems that had developed from an earlier law to discourage trafficking in minors and allow for the expedited return of unaccompanied minors and then defund DACCA. And, of course, that Obama should enforce immigration laws as written. These proposals are discussed in this Heritage article by David Insure:

C3-AK
https://www.heritage.org/immigration/report/children-illegally-crossing-the-us-border-responding-requires-policy-changes

No such suggested policy changes were followed.

Other border-related issues

Public health

Legal immigration procedures require health information to prevent importation of communicable diseases. There is no such protocol for those entering illegally. Many diseases that were virtually banished, or occurred in lower numbers than in less medically advanced times, have been increasing in occurrence in recent years. This 2016 post by Matthew Vaduz in the Americans for Legal Immigration blog describes a problem made worse by Obama's easy-entry practices:

C3-AL https://www.alipac.us/f12/obamas-refugees-surging-deadly-diseases-america-332955/#post
and Furious

Fast and Furious

"Operation Fast and Furious," was designed to help the

Bureau of Alcohol, Tobacco, Firearms, and Explosives (AFT) dismantle drug cartels operating inside the United States and disrupt drug-trafficking routes. Instead, it put into the hands of criminals south of the border some 2,000 weapons, which have been used to kill hundreds of Mexicans and at least one American, a U.S. Border Patrol agent. The project might also have been initiated to promote a call for more gun control, as all the weapons were obtained (with coordination from AFT) from Arizona gun stores.

In November 2009, the ATM's Phoenix field office launched an operation in which guns bought by drug-cartel straw purchasers in the U.S. were allowed to "walk" across the border into Mexico. AFT agents would then track the guns as they made their way through the ranks of the cartel. Not surprisingly, once the guns moved across the border, they were out of U.S. sight. Whistleblowers reported, and investigators later confirmed, that the AFT made no effort to trace the guns.

The results were deadly. A good description of what went wrong and of the obstinate resistance of Justice to admit its errors can be found in this article by Ian Tutee appearing in National Review in 2016 after one of the F&F guns were discovered in drug lord Joaquin "El Chap Gunman's hideaway:

C3-AM http://www.nationalreview.com/article/430153/fast-furious-obamas-first-scandal

It is difficult, too, to overstate the contempt of this regime for transparency, given that, having made those fatal mistakes, its response was to hide them from a congressional inquiry, going so far as to invoke executive privilege to do so. In June 2012, Congress voted to hold Holder in contempt of Congress. Alas, in the fall of 2014 he got a federal judge to reverse the holding. At best, the operation and its aftermath were an exercise in astonishing malpractice; at worst, the Obama regime knowingly exhibited a reckless disregard for human life and then covered it up.

Feckless foreign policy

Several themes appear in reviewing Obama's approach to foreign policy. Among them are "Leading from behind," a pro-Muslim tilt and aversion to use of the military.

"Leading from behind" is a term a White House official coined in 2011 to describe Obama's approach to Libya, where he and Hillary replaced a government that had stopped actively working at cross purpose to the U.S. with a fractured, inefficient, and more stridently Islamic one.

Other examples of leading from behind would be the early exit from Iraq, the "reset" with Russia at the start of the first term, and avoiding strong measures that might have led to the removal of Basher al-Assay from Syria. The retreat from leadership in foreign disruptions that affected the U.S. and allies is surveyed in this 2015 article by the Heritage Foundation's James Jay Carrion:

C3-AN https://www.heritage.org/global-politics/commentary/obamas-lead-behind-strategy-has-us-full-retreat

Obama's pro-Muslim tilt was especially evident in his dealings with Israel and her hostile neighbors. An example is his direction to his United Nations ambassador, Samantha Power, not to veto an anti-Israel resolution regarding construction in the West Bank and East Jerusalem in 2016. The Palestinian Authority hailed "a day of Victory." And he bent over backwards to please Iran.

Obama was disposed to avoid using military power when the threat of use might have been persuasive. He unilaterally withdrew from Iraq, conducted a show surge in Afghanistan, created a void of U.S. influence in the Syrian civil war, backed down from his "red line" on Syria's use of chemical weapons, offered but a meek protest to Putin after Russia annexed Crimea, and did nothing to stop Chinese island-making in the South China Sea or counter nuclear weapon and ballistic missile development in North Korea. Nor was he able to get American hostages held abroad returned without a ransom or making a bad deal.

To follow are some specific situations in foreign or military matters where his decisions were not in the interest of the U.S.

Russian uranium grab

One result of newly appointed Secretary of State Hillary Clinton's "reset button" play to smooth over lingering differences between Russia and the Bush regime was a massive fix that ended up with Russia interests acquiring control over a fifth of U.S. uranium reserves.

It started with a $500,000 fee paid by a Kremlin-tied Russian bank for a 2010 speech by husband Bill, part of a multi-million-dollar influence-peddling scheme to enrich the Clintons and their foundation to the tune of $145 million. Russia was seeking U.S. government approval for its acquisition of a Canadian firm, Uranium One, and with it 20% of American uranium resources. State was one of the U.S. departments or agencies that needed to sign off on the deal.

Nothing surprising here for the Clintons: just another cashing in on pubic positions. But the Obama regime was knowingly compromising American national-security interests. The regime ended up making possible the transfer of control over a meaningful share of American uranium-mining capacity to Russia via its state-controlled nuclear-energy conglomerate, Rosatom, whose American subsidiary was engaged in a lucrative racketeering enterprise that had already committed felony extortion, fraud, and money-laundering offenses. The full story, and a chart of the players, can be found at this 2018 Epoch Times article:

C3-AO
https://www.theepochtimes.com/infographic-the-uranium-one-scandal_2436825.html

Potential terrorist not watched

At the 2013 Boston Marathon, two pressure-cooker bombs exploded near the finish line, killing three race watchers and injuring 264 others, including sixteen who lost limbs. As a resident of the Boston area, I can attest to the unsettling distress inflicted on all.

Good police work enabled the FBI, three days later, to identify two brothers of Kyrgyzstan origin as the attackers. The younger brother, Dzhokhar, was caught, convicted and sentenced to death in a federal trial.

The older brother, Tamerlan Tsarnaev, was killed in a shootout with police a few days after the bombing. He had been known to Obama's FBI since 2011, when it was informed by Russia that he was a potential terrorist who had just visited

Chechnya, a region known for Islamist training camps. Tamerlan was interviewed by the FBI, but the end result may not only have been failure to monitor and alert local authorities, but — according to a reporter with deep ties to Boston area law enforcement, Michele McPhee— his being protected in a new role as an FBI informer. This 2017 Who What Why book review outlines the case:

C3-AP https://whowhatwhy.org/2017/04/14/new-book-claims-fbi-obstructed-justice-boston-bombing/

Refusal to acknowledge domestic "radical Islamic terrorism"

On November 5, 2009 Nidal Hasan, a U.S. Army major and psychiatrist, fatally shot 13 people and injured more than 30 others at Fort Hood, Texas. Days after the shooting, reports in the media revealed that a Joint Terrorism Task Force had been aware of a series of e-mails between Hasan and Imam Anwar al-Awlaki, who had been monitored by the NSA as a security threat, and that Hasan's colleagues had been aware of his increasing radicalization for several years. In spite of the obvious connection with Islamic terrorism, the regime declined requests from survivors and family members of the slain to categorize the Fort Hood shooting as an act of terrorism, or motivated by militant Islamic religious convictions. Obama tagged it "workplace violence."

Osama raid aftermath

The May 2011 raid in Pakistan that took out Osama Bin Laden is one of those operations details of which are best kept secret lest the team becomes known and vulnerable to a hostile response. But Obama was up for re-election next year, so it didn't take long for details to be released and for the White House to feed information to a producer planning a movie on the raid. An organization concerned with keeping special operations details secret for the protection of personnel involved in such operations, OPEC, describes its concern about the urge for publicity by the Obama team in this case and other operations in this time period on its website:

C3-AQ
https://www.opsecteam.org/background.html

Three months after the Bin Laden raid, a transport helicopter carrying Seal Team Six members was shot down while on a mission in Afghanistan. Thirty Seals were killed. Was someone in the Afghan government seeking revenge for the Bin Laden raid? If the identity of the team that carried out the Bin Laden raid had not been released, there might not have been this target for our enemies to focus on. This 2013 Washington Times article describes the concerns of parents of team members:

C3-AR
https://www.washingtontimes.com/news/2013/oct/2
0/families-suspect-seal-team-6-crash-was-inside-
job-/

There is also a possibility that the name of the Pakistani doctor who conducted the vaccination ruse to confirm the location of Bin Laden was leaked by the regime, for reasons unknown. This Daily Mail story outlines the case:

C3-AS http://www.dailymail.co.uk/news/article-2149619/Shackle-Afraid-Obama-accused-aban-doning-Pakistani-doctor-led-Navy-SEALs-bin-Laden.html

Dr. Afraid was sentenced to 33 years in prison.

Turning tail in Iraq

To station forces in a host country it is necessary to have an understanding of how troops will be treated by the local legal system. Thus a Status of Forces Agreement must be worked out. In 2011 the State Department sought to negotiate a status of forces agreement with Iraq ahead of a planned partial withdrawal; the key question was one of immunity under Iraqi law for remaining U.S. forces. Iraqi Prime Minister Nor al-Malice was willing to grant them immunity, but the newly installed Obama regime then insisted the Iraqi parliament confirm this understanding. This step was politically untenable in the newly reorganized government of Iraq. So without an agreement Obama withdrew all U.S. forces, except for a few advisers.

That left a country not ready to adjust to the new realities that the U.S. invasion brought. A transition period aided by a residual U.S. force might have prevented or minimized the serious internal and, later, external problems presented when the brutal Islamic State took over large areas of the country, executed hundreds and enslaved the communities. Rick Brennan, a senior political scientist at the AND Corporation who served as senior adviser to the U.S. military in Iraq from 2006 to 2011, describes the folly of Obama's total troop withdrawal in this 2014 Foreign Affairs article:

C3-AT
https://www.foreignaffairs.com/articles/united-states/withdrawal-symptoms

Lunacy in Libya

After the Bin Laden raid, Obama wanted to convey the notion that the threat from

Al-Qaeda was over. But as we would learn in Libya, that was not the case. In the wake of the Arab Spring uprisings in 2011, the Obama regime intervened militarily to overthrow Libya's strongman, Mummer al-Gaddafi. This war action was without any input from Congress, and of questionable connection with the post-911 Congressional resolutions.

Some observers considered it to be a violation of the 1973 War Powers Act. In any case, no planning was evident for what would come after Gaddafi. The result was a mess, split between two major governing factions (and a swarm of minor ones) and ineptly run by all.

On September 11, 2012 the consulate and a CIA post in Benghazi were attacked by jihadists with mortars. Four Americans were killed, including the saxophone playing Ambassador J. Christopher Stevens, an idealistic proponent of encouraging the development of representative government in the post-Gaddafi Libya. Stephen was charged with establishing good relations with the faction ruling in the Benghazi area that the U.S. assumed was likely to eventually run the country. He refused to cower behind the embassy walls, even in as dangerous country as Libya. The other Americans were privately retained security personnel who went to defend the outpost even though State, after the attack had started, issued orders to stand down.

The official take was that the assault was a spontaneous reaction to a trailer for an amateur anti-Muslim video posted on YouTube in July. Private communications from secretary of state Clinton revealed that she knew it was a planned attack. But the elections were only two months away, so the lie about the motivation for the attack had to be perpetuated, lest voters have doubts about Obama as the terrific terminator of terrorists.

Also very wrong here is why no aid was given to the CIA post even though military assets were not far away. A select committee in Congress was eventually formed. Due to stonewalling by the regime, many questions were not answered, such as where was Obama during the siege and why were these outposts sited in a very dangerous area? But the Committee's report did reveal a staggering dereliction of duty and deception by the president and his top aides. A 2016 article in the Federalist by Mollie Hemingway summarizes the main conclusions of the report:

> C3-AU http://thefederalist.com/2016/06/28/5-big-takeaways-from-the-house-benghazi-report/

But one of the most shameful offenses was the treatment of the video maker, whom Obama asked the L.A. police to arrest on a minor parole violation. This 2015 article in American Thinker by Jack Cashill describes the unfair treatment by callous self-serving top officials in the Obama regime.

> C3-AV
> https://www.americanthinker.com/articles/2015/10/
> hilla-
> rys_worst_crime_was_against_the_filmmaker.html

Election meddling in Israel

Obama's dislike of Israel Prime Minister Benjamin (Bibi) Netanyahu was widely known; he wanted a more pro-Palestine, dovish successor. On Netanyahu's first visit to the White House in 2010, Obama presented a list of thirteen demands and pressed hardest on getting the Israeli PM to agree to halt residential building in east Jerusalem.

Netanyahu refused to commit to this demand, so Obama walked out of the meeting for an hour to have dinner with Michelle and the girls. Obama also refused to agree to a joint statement and forbade photographs of the meeting. In 2015 Obama childishly refused to meet with Netanyahu when he was in Washington to address a joint session of Congress.

It is amusing to hear complaints about putative meddling in the 2016 elections by Russia, while ignoring Obama's definite meddling in the 2015 Israeli elections. Obama arranged for U.S. funds to support OneVoice Israel and OneVoice Palestine, organizations designed to rally all other parties into one voting bloc against incumbent Bibi. This article in a 2015 article by Barry Shaw in the Jerusalem Post describes this most improper intrusion into an ally's electoral process:

C3-AW https://www.jpost.com/Blogs/The-View-from-Israel/Obamas-shocking-interference-into-Israels-election-process-389858

Perilous prisoner swap

In June of 2009, American soldier Robert "Bowe" Bergdahl went missing from his post in Afghanistan and was captured by the Taliban-affiliated Haqqani network. Early searches for him resulted in six deaths of U.S. soldiers, but the searches ended when it was clear that Bergdahl had walked away from his unit. The Taliban from time to time released videos of their captive with his pleas for the U.S. to withdraw. In 2011, after U.S. Special Forces killed Osama bin Laden, U.S. officials re-ignited discussions on how to bring back Bergdahl, a goal more of interest to the White House than the Army.

By early 2014 there was increasing pressure from some quarters to strike a deal to recover Bergdahl. One problem was a recent understanding with Congress to get a 30-day notice of any planned Guantanamo Bay (Gitmo) prisoner releases, as Obama had been seen as too inclined to release without careful consideration of the risks. The Taliban had long demanded the release of five key commander detainees from Gitmo. And in May of 2014, despite resistance from some advisers, Obama agreed to exchange the five for Bergdahl, despite the Congressional restriction. Many were appalled at the lack of balance in the trade, given the high level of the released Taliban commanders. Sen. Lindsay Graham (R-S.C.) said that Republicans might start thinking about impeachment if more prisoners are released from Guantanamo. Bergdahl's home town in Idaho decided to cancel their homecoming event after its officials learned more about his desertion.

In 2015, Obama tried to portray Bergdahl as a war hero, and invited his parents to the Rose Garden to celebrate the news of his release. Obama maintained he only freed five Taliban leaders to free a soldier who, in the words of his National Security Adviser Susan Rice, "served the United States with honor and distinction."

But the Pentagon refused to list Bergdahl as a POW, because

an internal 2009 Army report found he had a history of walking off his posts, and more than likely had deserted. It also found he had shipped his laptop back home to Idaho, and left a note expressing his disillusionment with the war. Certainly Obama had access to this intelligence long before he made his swap deal. But maybe he saw the trade as one more notch in his obsession with closing down Gitmo.

Getting chummy with the Castros

In late 2014, for absolutely no improvement in civil liberties or other concessions, Obama decided to re-normalize relations with the communist dictatorship of Cuba. But the Castro regime did not let up in its repression; in 2015 it arrested between 150-200 dissidents on Human Rights Day. Also, on Sundays regime-organized mobs still blocked a brave group of women relatives of jailed dissidents known as the Ladies in White from marching after church services. These women are always insulted, often beaten and occasionally arrested. And there was a revived crackdown on churches and religious groups.

The repression will likely continue after the both brothers die, as they have put family members in key government and business positions, like Castro's son-in-law, General Luis Alberto Rodriguez who controls an estimated 90% of the Cuban economy through the holding company he heads.

Admiration of dictators is nothing new for American liberals. After all, they both favor the big state. Of Raul Castro, Obama said "I do see in him a big streak of pragmatism. In that sense, I don't think he is an ideologue." But many regard Raul as the more ideologically committed and ruthless of the Castro brothers. The re-normalization was bad enough, but in March 2016

Obama traveled to Cuba to pay homage to the junta and perhaps to make the recognition harder for a later regime to reverse.

The 2018 Freedom House rating for freedom in Cuba is worse (6.7/7) than for 2014 (6.5/7), the year Obama decided that Cuba was just fine:

C3-AX https://freedomhouse.org/report/freedom-world/2018/cuba

Another agreement in lieu of a treaty: Iran

It was evident before Obama's tenure that Iran was developing nuclear capability well beyond what would be needed for electric power. Obama was pressured internally and by allies to do something to curtail or remove their ability to develop nuclear weapons by controlling production of enriched uranium. With the five permanent members of the U.N. Security Council and the E.U., a "Joint Comprehensive Plan of Action" agreement was reached in mid-2015.

In return for relief from sanctions, it called for Iran to reduce or eliminate uranium stockpiles, centrifuges and heavy-water plants and be subject to inspections. After ten years some of these restrictions would disappear, and after fifteen years there would be no restraints.

There were several problems here. One, the Agreement was not a treaty, so the Senate never was asked for its ratification. Two, the International Atomic Energy Agency did not have a good record of catching violations of previous understandings in Iran and Sadam Hussein's Iraq. Three, after ten and fifteen years, were we to expect that Iran would no longer be ruled by this regime or one with a similar yearning for nuclear weapons?

Fortunately, a U.S. law required periodic certification of compliance, which for good reason Trump refused to do in October 2017, setting the stage for his withdrawal from the Agreement in March 2018. But the takeaway is that, for whatever reason, Obama wanted to give Iran a deal short on teeth.

Bad bargain: pallets of cash and an uneven swap of prisoners

At the time the Agreement was finalized, Iran held five Americans for various real and imagined charges and the U.S. held seven U.S.-based undercover arms procurers for Iran, discovered by an extensive investigation over several years. There was no equivalence here.

Perhaps to make the six-party Agreement deal look more attractive to Americans, Obama persuaded Iran to make this swap by a disturbing incentive: piles of Euros and other non-U.S. currency stacked on pallets, $1.7 billion in all, delivered by a non-U.S. aircraft before dawn.

When this transfer was discovered, the official story was that this was the sum due Iran from a down payment (plus interest) made by the Shah's government for military goods that were never delivered due to the 1979 Islamic Revolution. Even if that was the whole story, the timing was too close to the hostage release to appear other than a ransom, which is against long-standing U.S. policy.

But any amount owed to Iran was uncertain as the U.S. had filed an $817 million counterclaim for Iran's violations of its obligations under the Pentagon's Foreign Military Sales (FMS) account. Further diminishing Iran's claim was a 2000 law, The

Victims of Trafficking and Violence Protection Act, which specified that Iran's FMS account could not be refunded until court judgments held by the U.S. government against Iran for damages from terrorist acts against American citizens were resolved to America's satisfaction. Both channels when fully applied could mean that Iran owed the U.S.!

So in making this payment to Iran, Obama both ignored the law and made American taxpayers cover the damages owed by Iran for its acts of terrorism against American citizens. And by returning this down payment, Obama and Kerry gave up almost everything the U.S. had to offer, just to secure a weak nuclear deal. Thus the U.S. had almost no leverage to address other issues, such as Iran's missile development and aggressive interference with other countries in the region.

For more insight as to the money aspect of this prisoner swap, visit this article in The Tablet:

C3-AY
https://www.tabletmag.com/scroll/255932/the-obama-regimes-1-7-billion-iranian-deception

For more detail about the imbalance between the sides on the prisoner swap, visit this 2017 Politico article by Josh Meyer:

C3-AZ http://www.polit-ico.com/story/2017/04/24/obama-iran-nuclear-deal-prisoner-release-236966

Letting Hezbollah off the hook

In the year before Obama was first inaugurated, the Drug Enforcement Agency (DEA) launched an effort to undercut Hezbollah funding from illicit drug sources. Project Cassandra investigated the terrorist organization's funding and the DEA concluded that Hezbollah had become increasingly involved with drug trafficking and organized crime to raise funds for its activities. Their investigations tracked how large sums of money were being laundered from the Americas, through Africa, to Lebanon, then into Hezbollah's coffers.

Egged on early in his term by John Brennan (who admitted voting for the Communist candidate in the 1976 presidential election), then assistant for Homeland Security and counterterrorism and later CIA director, Obama looked for ways to increase "moderate elements" in Hezbollah. As his desire grew to negotiate a deal concerning Iran's nuclear program, his willingness to view its ally, Hezbollah, in a better light than evidenced by reality led to a suspension of meaningful efforts by Project Cassandra leaders to identify the source of drug money going to Hezbollah. Again, Josh Meyer in Politico spills the beans:

> C3-BA http://www.politico.com/interactives/2017/obama-hezbollah-drug-trafficking-investigation/

The Paris Agreement

The 2016 "Paris Agreement" is a deal within the United Nations Framework Convention on Climate Change (UNFCCC), dealing with greenhouse-gas-emissions mitigation, adaptation, and finance, starting in the year 2020. The stated goal was to keep the increase in global average temperature to below 1.5C to substantially reduce the risks and effects of climate change. Under the Agreement, each country is to determine plan, and regularly report on the contribution that it undertook to mitigate global warming. But there was no mechanism to force a country to set a specific target by a specific date.

According to a 2017 comprehensive study prepared by NERA Economic Consulting, meeting the commitments President Obama made as part of this accord could have cost the U.S. economy $3 trillion and 6.5 million industrial sector jobs by 2040, The study was commissioned by the American Council for Capital Formation with support from the U.S. Chamber of Commerce Institute for 21st Century Energy. The full report is at

C3-BB
https://www.eenews.net/assets/2017/03/16/doc
ument_gw_02.pdf

Like the Iran nuclear agreement, Obama did not seek ratification from the Senate, even though it really was a treaty, as pointed out in a 2016 press release from Wyoming senators Mike Enzi and John Barrasso:

C3-BC
https://www.enzi.senate.gov/public/index.cfm/2
016/11/president-obama-doesn-t-speak-for-
congress-on-climate-agreement

Fortunately, president Trump took the U.S. out of the Agreement in mid-2017. Brett Schaefer writing for The Daily Signal explains that this decision was a good move, as it forced attention to the importance of Senate ratification of such agreements:

C3-BD
https://www.dailysignal.com/2017/06/08/trump-
right-leave-paris-agreement-shouldnt-withdraw-
first-place/

Neglected threats

"Studied avoidance" might be the best way to describe the way in which Obama dealt with several difficult, long-standing and new security threats.

North Korea

While all presidents since Eisenhower and before Obama failed to bring down the government of the Democratic People's Republic of Korea (DPRK) or keep its bellicosity in check, the path to substantial nuclear capability accelerated during the Obama regime. Kim Jong-il wasted no time reinvigorating the DPRK's nascent nuclear weapons program following Obama's taking office. In April 2009 North Korea announced that it would never again take part in six-party type talks and would not be bound by any agreement reached at the talks. It also expelled nuclear inspectors, informed the International Atomic Energy Agency that it would resume their nuclear weapons program, and announced that they had reactivated their nuclear facilities. In May they tested their second nuclear device.

In Obama's last year in office, the DPRK conducted their fourth and fifth nuclear tests. Director of National Intelligence James Clapper, an Obama appointee, said on an October 2016 BBC program that persuading North Korea to abandon its nuclear program is probably a lost cause since to them it was their "ticket to survival" and any discussions about ending their nuclear ambitions would be a "non-starter."

The great wall of sand

Almost as serious, especially for world trade, was the Chinese island-creating venture in the South China Sea during the Obama regime. To strengthen territorial claims to atolls and reefs, the PRC embarked on large-scale land-building projects on atolls in 2013 and subsequently built structures, including landing strips, on some of the new islands.

Pictures taken in these man-made islands and the structures built on them can be found at this 2018 New York Times site:

C3-BE
https://www.nytimes.com/2018/02/08/world/asia/so
uth-china-seas-photos.html

Though the pre-Communist Republic of China had promulgated a 1948 map that claimed most of the South China Sea beyond a nine-mile zone off other countries' coast, no serious moves to grab territory had been made until the Obama years. Other countries nearer to the atolls and reefs later grabbed by PRC, have equally valid claims. The whole area is a huge waterway through which substantial international sea traffic pass every year. According to the ChinaPower think tank, $3.4 trillion of trade passed through the South China Sea in 2016.

C3-BF https://chinapower.csis.org/much-trade-
transits-south-china-sea/

In 2016 The Permanent Court of Arbitration (PCA) in The Hague delivered a rebuke to China's aggressions in the region. Under the Law of the Sea Treaty, it ruled that China's claim to sovereignty over the South China Sea has no legal basis, condemned China's continued construction of artificial islands and stated firmly that China had violated Philippine rights in grabbing Scarborough Shoal. But China condemned the PCA decision and continued building.

In part, the South China Sea became such a zone of tension because the Obama regime was loath to back the legitimate claims of other countries to the islands and reefs. The Obama regime was also ambiguous about asserting the right of free passage around the islands China has claimed. It did send two carrier groups into the Western Pacific. But show-the-flag sails near the new Chinese-held islands by U.S. Navy vessels to assert the principle of freedom of passage were sporadic and ambiguous. And Obama made little effort to force China to reverse its militarizing moves.

In this 2016 Guardian article Simon Tisdall explains the long-term consequences of Obama's abrogation of this issue:

C3-BG
https://www.theguardian.com/commentisfree/2016/sep/25/obama-failed-asian-pivot-china-ascendant

Conflicted response to Syrian civil war

Perhaps the worst humanitarian crisis of the 21st century so far was Bashar al-Assad's long war against his own people. It saw a half a million killed in Syria, millions of refugees fleeing to Jordan, Turkey, and Lebanon, and millions internally displaced. The overflow from the Syrian refugee crisis threatened to destabilize Europe. There are strategic issues too, as American allies on Syria's borders, including Israel, must now be concerned about keeping Iran and Hezbollah from opening a new front on the Syrian side of the Golan Heights.

So why did Obama not make any serious effort to contain Assad —such as implementing a no-fly regime or supplying the rebels with anti-aircraft gear? Or even just establishing an internal refugee camp adjacent to the border with Turkey? Most likely because U.S. intervention in Syria would have nixed his nuclear deal with Iran.

This conclusion is evident from a December 2015 press conference, where Obama spoke of "respecting" Iranian "equities" in Syria. In other words, leaving Assad alone in order to keep Iranian leaders pleased. The connection between Syria and the Iran deal was not particularly hard to spot.

Some insight into Obama's thinking is revealed in a 2016 book *The Iran Wars* by Jay Solomon (Penguin Books) in which he relates that Iranian officials told him that even had the diplomats doing the negotiations wanted to stay in talks, the Islamic Revolutionary Guard Corps would have pulled the plug if Obama intervened in Syria. He also related that Obama sent a letter to Khamenei saying he wouldn't target Assad and Pentagon officials told him they were concerned that operations in Syria risked undermining the nuclear negotiations.

David Greenberg observes the shortcomings of Obama's Syrian policy in this December 2016 Foreign Policy article:

> C3-BH https://foreignpol-
> icy.com/2016/12/29/obama-never-understood-how-
> history-works/

Greenberg disparages Obama's not realizing the Syria was of great strategic importance to the United States and not seeing the massive implications should Russia displace the United States as the region's preeminent great power. America's access to energy, its ability to fight terrorism, and its capacity to ensure Israel's survival were all at stake as well as the implications of Obama's Syria policy on Europe's immigration crisis.

~4~
Social and Moral Issues

For better or worse, presidents can affect the values and norms of society. The Obama legacy in social issues was hugely negative for those who value natural, bottom-up development of social mores based on what kind of society the people prefer to create and live in, and who communicate such norms to their legislators where laws are appropriate to maintain these norms.

Failure to enforce drug laws

The president is the chief federal law enforcement officer. And where there is a conflict federal law supersedes state or local laws, provided the enforcement action falls within the Constitutionally enumerated federal powers. So when a president allows its Justice Department to accede to a state's legalizing an activity that remains illegal federally, is not such a president failing to carry out his office?

Early in the Obama regime, its Justice Department issued the Odgen Memo that reduced the threat of enforcement of cannabis laws for medical uses of marijuana, which some states had legalized. But that was not enough for the Rocky Mountain state, whose voters approved an amendment referendum in 2012 calling for legalizing recreational use of cannabis. Obama's Justice Department retreated and in 2013 issued a memo from assistant attorney general James Cole that the Feds would not strictly enforce cannabis laws in states that had legalized recreational use subject to a "robust system" of restrictions, such as controlling cultivation, distribution and sale and possession, and the implementing of measures to prevent diversion of marijuana outside the regulated system and to other states.

So how are things in Colorado since legalization? Governor Hickenlooper is having doubts, as related in this 2018 CNN story.

C4-AA
https://www.cnn.com/2018/04/20/us/colorado-
marijuana-and-crime/index.html

But the most serious adverse consequence of Obama's abandonment of enforcing federal law is the legal confusion and opportunity for mischief for other areas of life where a state might be now tempted to deviate on its own. If the federal law is no longer one seen as the correct policy by most Americans, then the political process should be allowed to proceed to its abolition. But until that happens, the federal government should uniformly enforce federal laws.

Gutting of 1996 welfare reform

The 1996 welfare reform law, which Clinton signed under pressure from the Republican Congress, strengthened work requirements of the Temporary Assistance for Needy Families

(TANF) program. But in 2012, Obama had a policy directive released by the Department of Health and Human Services that allowed states to waive the TANF program's work requirements, even though Congress had never granted such waiver authority to any department. So by this action he helped recreate the environment that was so destructive to the certain poor communities, especially black. The Heritage Foundation's Robert Rector explains the folly of this action in this 2017 article:

C4-AB
https://www.heritage.org/welfare/commentary/oba
ma-gutted-work-requirements-welfare-why-trump-
right-restore-them

Commenting on same-sex marriage

A president can have a large influence on the culture, for better or worse. It was during the Obama regime that a huge change —forced top-down by agencies of the federal government— occurred in American social norms: the legitimization of same-sex marriage. Though it was a later very badly decided Supreme Court decision that ushered in "the love that dare not speak its name" as just another choice, the comments of Obama certainly must have contributed to bringing about this denaturalization of a standard convention of organized society in every civilized society as far as is known to history.

Before becoming president, Obama said that same-sex marriage was against his religious beliefs and something that should be in the hands of churches rather than government. In 2008, he said: "I believe marriage is between a man and a woman. I am not in favor of gay marriage."

In May 2012, on a Meet the Press program, Joe Biden allowed that he "is absolutely comfortable with . . . men marrying men, women marrying women." Was this just another Biden gaffe? Or did Obama suggest it as a trial balloon to pave the way for his own statement later that year, when he said in an interview "I've just concluded that for me personally it is important for me to go ahead and affirm that I think same-sex couples should be able to get married."?

The *Obergefell v. Hodges* decision, which overrode by judicial fiat state powers in regard to marriage, came three years later. What influence did earlier comments from the White House have on the five justices conflating the former-slave protections of the 14th Amendment with the creation of a new "right" that conflicted with state laws, and the devolved sense of a society as the way things ought to be for its most important social institution?

Social engineering in the military

Distaff delusions

While women have been involved with the U.S. military in various non-combat roles for generations, it was in the Obama regime that took things to an absurd and potentially dangerous level. In 2013 departing Defense Secretary Leon Panetta announced that women would henceforth be a candidate for every duty, including combat infantry. David Frum, writing in The Daily Beast, applies his knowledge of recent developments with much common sense in this article that describes both the practical and social implications of women in fighting roles:

<u>C4-AC</u> https://www.thedailybeast.com/the-truth-about-women-in-combat

A court ruling in 1978 overturned statutes that prohibited women from serving on other-than-hospital ships. Obama pushed hard to increase the number, despite that the likely consequence would be pregnant sailors. In early 2017 the Navy reported that a record 16 out of 100 Navy women in 2016 were reassigned from ship to shore duty due to pregnancy. This information was discovered from a FOIA request by the Daily Caller in 2017. The details are in this story:

<u>C4-AD</u> http://dailycaller.com/2017/03/01/exclusive-deployed-us-navy-has-a-pregnancy-problem-and-its-getting-worse/

Pregnancy wasn't the only problem. Seeing increasing sexual assaults, the Pentagon in 2014 commissioned a RAND corporation study which revealed that females serving on ships and at large training bases were at the greatest risk for sexual assault. The highest assault rate was at the U.S. Naval base in Charleston, S.C. where 17% of females reported that they had been sexually assaulted; followed by women on ships, especially aircraft carriers. The study was released in the fall of 2018. A summary can be seen below:

<u>C4-AE</u>
https://www.rand.org/pubs/research_reports/RR87
0z7.html

Obama even pushed for women to serve on submarines, despite having to replace some ordnance zones to create separate berthing areas. And most misguided of all, he pushed for women to join the Navy Seals, clearly a male domain. One female enlisted in 2017 but withdrew while in training. As of this writing no female has completed the training.

Ending Don't Ask, Don't Tell (DADT)

Don't Ask Don't Tell was a Clinton revision of military policy that changed the previous long-standing prohibition of homosexuals in the services. It allowed for homosexuals to serve, as long as they kept their proclivities private. Having served in the Navy (well before DADT) I cannot imagine having avowed and out homosexuals in the close quarters of life in the service. The respect for comrades in arms necessary for a force to function well, especially in combat, could be dangerously short in such an environment.

But the open-and-out Obama policy might be a case of his misconstruing military service as a right, rather than a conclusion that this modification of personnel policy would make no difference in effective functioning. Carson Holloway in The Witherspoon Institute's Public Discourse explains the misunderstanding of "rights" in this decision:

C4-AF http://www.thepublicdiscourse.com/2010/02/1139/

Pushing the "trans" agenda

In his last year in office, Obama decided to entertain gender dysphoria in members of the military by ordering the government to pay for "sex change" operations (not that an operation can actually change one's sex) rather than continue the sensible policy of discharge. Aside from the expense of the operation, there is the cost of pay for no work during an extensive procedure and recovery, and the stress on others of dealing daily with a company member who is not sure of who they really are or may not be thinking clearly. One sensible member of Congress, Vicky Hartzler (R-Missouri) spoke out on this nonsense:

C4-AG
https://www.kansascity.com/news/local/news-columns-blogs/the-buzz/article159090809.html

The military is there to defend the country, not to be a place for social experiments and being admitted to its ranks is not a right. Any policies that lessen the effectiveness of the military, or generate unnecessary costs, will diminish our security.

Suppressing the military vote

In the 2008 election, an unusually low percentage of overseas military submitted absentee ballots, so Congress passed the Overseas Voter Empowerment Act to better ensure that all members of the military have a chance to vote. But Obama's Pentagon seemed to ignore this law in the 2012 elections by not getting military absentee ballots to where they were needed in time or sufficient number. Rick Ungar in a September 2012 article in Forbes describes the effort to disenfranchise voters, whom Obama surely viewed in the aggregate as more likely to vote Republican than Democrat:

C4-AH
https://www.forbes.com/sites/rickungar/2012/09/26/obama-accused-of-suppressing-military-vote-by-withholding-absentee-ballots/

Increasing racial divide

In 2008 a common view was that the election of a black president would soothe race relations. But after his eight years it seems to this observer that the racial divide became larger, not smaller. Several polls near the end of his last term support this impression. For example, this July, 2016 Rasmussen poll report that 60% of likely voters think that race relations were worse since Obama's first election.

C4-AI http://www.rasmussenreports.com/public_content/politics/current_events/social_issues/60_say_race_relations_have_gotten_worse_since_obama_s_election

Perhaps this view was because Obama had a huge chip on his shoulder. That is, Obama thought of America more as place where whites were still oppressing blacks rather than a place, post slavery and post Jim-Crow laws, of opportunity for all. On many occasions, he saw disparities between groups as evidence of discrimination, then used all available resources to combat whites, men, police and Christians he saw as villains or actors from an unfair power center. John Gibbs at the Federalist Society describes well the development of the increased divide:

C4-AJ http://thefederalist.com/2016/07/13/how-obama-left-us-more-racially-divided-than-ever/

Bad mouthing entrepreneurs

Demonstrating gross ignorance of what creates wealth and raises income levels over time was Obama's obsession with the collective. In 2012 he gave a speech in which he ridiculed the idea that individuals can claim credit for their successes. "You didn't build that" was the key line.

In the below article, Emily Ekins of the Cato Institute explains how out of sync this view of government as provider and innovator is with the American public. An aggregate of polls on this question, she writes, suggests that upwards of 60% of Americans believe that hard work matters more than luck, inheritances or connections, whereas in Obama's world view a person's results in life have more to do with what others (read: government) do for them.

C4-AK https://rea-son.com/poll/2012/07/18/obamas-you-didnt-build-that-speec-out-of

I built my investment advisory business without any assistance (but with much regulation!) from government. This collectivist mentality is just not America as we have known it.

Proclivity to prevarication

All presidents lie from time to time, but Obama probably said more than his share. The below list of tall tales is a collection of some that come to mind:

> *The stimulus will fund shovel-ready jobs.*
>
> *The IRS is not targeting anyone.*
>
> *It was a spontaneous riot about a movie. The Cambridge cops acted stupidly.*
>
> *The public will have five days to look at every bill that lands on my desk.*
>
> *It's not my red line - it is the world's red line.*

85

Whistle blowers will be protected in my administration.

I am not spying on American citizens.

You can keep your family doctor. Premiums will be lowered by $2500.

If you like it, you can keep your current healthcare plan.

I knew nothing about "Fast and Furious" gunrunning to Mexican drug cartels.

I knew nothing about IRS targeting conservative groups.

I knew nothing about what happened in Benghazi.

I have never known my uncle from Kenya who is in the country illegally and that he was arrested and told to leave the country over 20 years ago.

And, I have never lived with that uncle. [He finally admitted (12-05-2013) that he DID know his uncle and that he DID live with him.]

Post-term arrogance

There won't be a presidential library in the usual manner, maintained by the National Archives. Rather, Obama wants a Center run by an Obama Foundation that will, it appears, house an Institute "that will enhance the pursuit of the President's initiatives beyond 2017." In seeking a Chicago location for his presidential library, Obama spotted a 20-acre park on the South Side. The selection of this site raised objections by neighbors, the City and the nearby University of Chicago. Other less prime locations would require less infrastructure changes (at the combined local and federal cost of $174 million) and not remove a park from current public use. For this valuable space the Foundation will pay only $1 in perpetuity. Richard Epstein of the Hoover Institution makes the case for a less ambitious and disruptive siting:

C4-AL
https://www.hoover.org/research/comeuppance-obamas-presidential-center

For further reading

The Scandalous Presidency of Barack Obama by Matt Margolis; 2018, Bombardier Books (Post Hill Press)

The Worst President in History: The Legacy of Barack Obama by Matt Margolis and Mark Noonan; 2018, Victory Books

The New Democrat by Loren Spivak; 2010, BoundLess Books
C4-AM https://www.amazon.com/New-Democrat-Spivack-Loren-Truth/dp/2000002803

You Lie!: The Evasions, Omissions, Fabrications, Frauds, and Outright Falsehoods of Barack Obama by Jack Cashill; 2017, Broadside Books.

For a detailed list of links on various Obama topics visit this compendium by Andrew Dart, innovator, advisor and prominent executive in the Asia-Pacific insurance industry, who takes pride in writing and publishing on topics ignored by the mainstream press.

<u>C4-AN</u> http://www.akdart.com/obama.html.

Part Two
The Patient Protection and Affordable Health Care Act of 2010

We know the act as ObamaCare. The road to it was a long one, filled with legislation and rulings that has paved the way to what may be the worst law created by Congress that is still in effect. Let's first visit the steps that led to an environment in which such a hugely un-American law could have been inflicted on the people. The first step was a court case in 1942 that may seem unconnected with insurance or healthcare, but enlarged considerably the scope of powers assumed by the federal government over commerce, the predicate for federal overreaches such as ObamaCare. Many other steps followed that diminished the chance for a nation-wide free market for individual healthcare insurance to develop. Massachusetts led the way to compulsion, followed by ObamaCare.

A way to end the compulsion and allow the natural development of a healthcare insurance market based or normal business practices and free of government coercion is outlined.

~5~
The Path to Increasing Statism in Healthcare

Wars have consequences, many of which are unexpected. The Second World War led to actions and laws that, unintentionally perhaps, made for substantial and mostly negative changes in the relationship between medical providers and their patients. And a platform from which proponents of big government could build an edifice of top-down supervision and diminished freedom.

World-War II developments

1942 Wickard v. Filburn

This Supreme Court decision dramatically increased the power of the federal government to regulate economic activity. The Court upheld the Agricultural Adjustment Act of 1938, which mandated quotas on wheat production to control supply and support price levels. The Interstate Commerce Clause of the

Constitution permits the Congress "to regulate Commerce with foreign Nations, and among the several States, and with the Indian Tribes." The Court decided that farmer Filburn's small extra wheat production for family consumption reduced the amount of wheat he would buy for chicken feed on the open market, which is traded nationally (interstate), and therefore, Filburn's production could be regulated by the federal government.

Wickard rendered a nullity the Constitution's enumeration of the federal government's limited powers. With just one of those powers, to regulate commerce among the states, it could now reach a host of activities.

Or non-activity as in the case of ObamaCare. In 2012, *Wickard* was central to arguments in *National Federation of Independent Business v. Sebelius* regarding the constitutionality of the individual mandate in ObmaCare. While the majority decision did acknowledge that the individual mandate did not fall within the power of Congress under the Commerce Clause, it did have such power by virtue of the penalties for not buying health insurance being a "capitation" (a head or poll tax), or a tax that everyone must pay simply for existing and that capitations are expressly contemplated by the Constitution.

Hence, the majority decision in *Sibelius* reflected the influence of *Wickard* —the twisted reasoning that the penalty was a tax notwithstanding. It is probable, had *Wickard* been decided in favor of farmer Filburn, that the compulsion in ObamaCare might never had been even considered by its drafters.

1942 National War Labor Board (NWLB)

In the U.S. medical insurance has come to be mostly

associated with employment. As far back as the 1920's, a few big employers had offered health insurance plans to some of their workers, but most people made their own healthcare arrangements, with or without insurance.

By World War II, with the United States now fully committed to the eradication of fascism, President Franklin Roosevelt wanted to prevent potential labor union strikes, which would slow industrial production and impede the war effort. The nation's urgent and massive conversion to a war economy and the dramatic increase in employment threatened to put labor unions and industrial leaders at odds over working conditions and wages. So Roosevelt issued an executive order creating the National War Labor Relations board in early 1942.

The NWLB was made up of political, business and labor leaders who were tasked with providing labor-policy recommendations. Although the NWLB was established to mediate between parties involved in industrial disputes, Roosevelt also gave the board power to intercede and impose settlements in order to preempt any pause in production. The following October, Roosevelt issued the Order Providing for the Stabilization of the National Economy, which expanded the NWLB's control over wages and prices by stipulating that any adjustment of wages had to be cleared through the Board. But the Order let employers circumvent the cap by offering "fringe benefits" —notably, health insurance. The fringe benefits created a huge tax subsidy, in that they were treated as tax-deductible expenses for corporations but no as taxable income for workers.

The result was revolutionary. Companies and unions quickly negotiated new health insurance plans. Some were run by Blue Cross, Blue Shield and private insurance companies. Others were "Taft-Hartley funds," run jointly by management and unions. By 1950, half of all companies with fewer than 250 workers and two-thirds of all companies with more than 250 workers offered health insurance of some kind.

But consider that the employee-benefit approach does nothing to address the healthcare needs of the unemployed. Even worse, it insulates consumers from the value of the healthcare they are paying for, giving them no incentive to economize, thereby driving up the cost of healthcare through demand push. And the employee-benefit system leads to "job lock," whereby people are afraid to leave their jobs if they fall ill, as switching plans could mean higher premiums or denial of coverage.

1945 The McCarran-Ferguson Act

Another development that helped disrupt a normal free market for health insurance was directly related to insurance. In six southern states The South-Eastern Underwriters Association controlled 90 percent of the market for fire and other insurance lines and was accused of setting rates at high, non-competitive levels. Eventually a suit, *United States v. South-Eastern Underwriters Association,* came before the Supreme Court in 1944 on appeal from the Atlanta district court.

The question before the Court was whether or not insurance was a form of "interstate commerce," which could be regulated under the Commerce Clause of the Constitution and the Sherman Anti-Trust Act. The general opinion in law before this case, according to the Court, was that the business of insurance was not commerce, and the District Court concurred with the opinion. In his partial dissent, Justice Robert H. Jackson noted that the conclusion that insurance was not commerce under the law rested with Congress, and that the Court should follow the lead of Congress.

As a result, in March of 1945, the McCarran-Ferguson Act was passed by Congress. Among other things, it:

> partially exempts insurance companies from the federal anti-trust legislation that applies to most businesses;

> allows states to regulate insurance;

> allows states to establish mandatory licensing requirements; and

> preserves certain state laws of insurance.

The main consequence of this law was to destroy a nationwide free market for insurance. We remember that one of the main reasons to call a convention in Philadelphia to reorganize the states under a new constitution was to facilitate interstate commerce. Under the Articles of Confederation states were free to levy customs and intrusive regulations that inhibited the free exchange of goods and, by extension, services.

But under the newly enshrined state-by-state structure, the only people who benefit may be the large body of state insurance regulators. Except for minor, temporary lines such as trip insurance, policy seekers are restricted to lines approved in their state. A state could have sensible regulations, or ones that raise the cost of policies without good reason, or discourage entry by a worthy underwriter.

Insurance is one of those industries that require a sophisticated analysis of risk exposure to set rates that will cover expected losses. It also requires competition to prevent imposition of excessive rates by other issuers of a particular line. State rate setting and imposition of mandatory coverages distort the math, create market inefficiencies and lessen the variety of insurance lines.

Massachusetts, for example

Let's look at automobile insurance. Perhaps the first move by organized society to deal with the financial results of auto accidents came with the compulsory liability insurance statute in Massachusetts in 1927, with the objective to make all parties financially responsible. Until 2008, Massachusetts set rates for automobile insurance; the results were that the number of firms offering coverage was limited and that the Commonwealth had the most expensive auto insurance rates in the country.

After rate setting ended in 2008, drivers started to save substantially. The change has helped attract numerous insurance companies to the state since 2008, even GEICO. Competition means that companies offer more features in their policies, like accident forgiveness and disappearing deductibles for safe drivers. No insurance companies had offered those features in Massachusetts before because there was no incentive.

Competition also means that agencies have to compete with insurers who sell policies online and advertise heavily. The companies now work harder to provide better service, such as helping customers save money, smoothing things out for them if there is a claim, or dealing with the motor vehicles department. Further, insurers can now offer discounts for customers having other lines of coverage with the same firm.

Now because automobile registration and driving laws are properly under state purview, there is naturally more state involvement in this line of insurance than others. The history of automobile insurance gestures towards a complex interplay of financial responsibility laws, compulsory insurance laws, and uninsured motorist coverage based largely on the principles of tort law. A tort occurs when someone either deliberately or through negligence harms another person or group. Thus, the concept of auto insurance is fundamentally a tort system.

Other lines of insurance

For other lines, detailed state supervision and regulation has driven up the cost of insurance. Likely, in many other states there would be more lines of insurance offered without the need to register and be subject to detailed supervision state by state.

Health insurance is where the most absurdities developed, owing in part to McCarran and the NWLR Board action. It is quite possible that some of the dysfunction and discomfort with health insurance that motivated government intrusion could have arisen from limited competition stemming from the need for insurers to register in each state —and from the often detailed state requirements for mandatory coverages and regulation of rates. And of course, in these situations there is always the possibility that local politicians and insurance executives could be paid-off.

In some states, such as in pre-RomneyCare Massachusetts, insurers were required to include all sorts of benefits in every policy such as mental health coverage and were limited in offerings of simple catastrophic policies. A shopper just wanting a straightforward policy covering potential future ailments was forced to buy, and pay for, an excessive package. A well-off buyer who could and wanted to self-insure for most of his likely medical expenses, but wanted to cover unexpected major expenses of a truly serious condition, was out of luck as many states had price controls on medical insurance under a variety of schemes and tables.

Post-war developments

1949 NLRB ruling upheld

In 1949, the U.S. Supreme Court let stand a lower court ruling that pensions, and by extension other employee benefits, were a "mandatory subject of bargaining" under the National Labor Relations Act. The *Inland Steel v. NLRB* ruling had the effect of reducing political pressure from organized labor and other groups to enhance government-provided retirement and healthcare benefits.

1954 The Revenue Act of 1954

This Act (Sec. 106) formally excludes from taxation employers' contributions to accident and health plans benefiting employees, and clarifies that such contributions had always been deductible as business expenses. The employee-benefit healthcare insurance system is thus further entrenched.

1986 to 1993 emergency medical care compulsion

The motivation for a national mandate-style healthcare scheme started with a piece of legislation passed in 1986 by a Democratic House and a Republican Senate and signed by President Ronald Reagan, called the Emergency Medical Treatment and Active Labor Act, or EMTALA. (EMTALA was passed as part of a larger budget bill called the Consolidated Omnibus

Budget Reconciliation Act, or COBRA, which is best known for allowing those who have lost their jobs to continue buying health insurance through their old employer's group plan.)

EMTALA, one of the greatest unfunded mandates in American history, required any hospital participating in Medicare (which is nearly all of them) to provide emergency care to anyone who needs it, including illegal immigrants, regardless of ability to pay. Indeed, EMTALA can be accurately said to have established universal healthcare in America, and without resistance from conservatives.

In response, there arose a worry about the "free rider" problem, in which people would intentionally go without health insurance, knowing that federal law required hospitals to care for them anyway.

In those days, most proposals for universal healthcare that were to the right of government-run single-payer were based upon forcing employers to sponsor private-sector health coverage for all of their employees. For example, under the Comprehensive Health Insurance Plan proposed by Richard Nixon in 1974, "every employer would be required to offer all full-time employees the Comprehensive Health Insurance Plan. Additional benefits could then be added by mutual agreement."

There are major problems with an employer mandate. One is that it massively drives up the cost of hiring new employees, thus discouraging new hiring. And forcing employers to pay for health costs increases the costs of running a business, which costs are passed onto consumers in the form of higher prices.

Unexpected move from the right

Hence, some conservatives, seeking a more market-oriented path to universal coverage, began endorsing an individual mandate over an employer mandate. An individual mandate was seen as a way to address the "free rider" problem caused by EMTALA, by requiring people to buy their own insurance. In addition, the thought was that moving to a more individual-based system from the employer-based one would significantly increase the efficiency of the health-insurance market.

With these considerations in mind, in 1989, Stuart Butler of the Heritage Foundation proposed a plan titled "Assuring Affordable Health Care for All Americans." Stuart's plan included a provision to "mandate all households to obtain adequate insurance" as a way to address both the free-rider problem and employer-mandate distortions. His underlying principle was that healthcare protection is a responsibility of individuals, not businesses. And since society one way or the other will provide essential care even if the afflicted cannot pay, it's just not right for an individual not to have coverage.

2006 RomneyCare

It is interesting that so many laws demonstrating bad economics come from leaders in the supposedly free-market party! Such is the case with the 2006 Massachusetts healthcare "reform" law: "An Act Providing Access to Affordable, Quality, Accountable Health Care," better known as RomneyCare, after its instigator, Massachusetts Republican Governor (2003-2007) Willard Mitt Romney. The reason to visit this state law is that it is the foundation and inspiration for ObamaCare. The heart of both is the individual mandate to obtain health insurance.

It seems that conservatives weren't concerned with the constitutional implications of allowing Congress to force people to buy a private product. In November 2004, for example, libertarian Ronald Bailey praised mandated private health insurance in *Reason* magazine, saying that it "could preserve and extend the advantages of a free market with a minimal amount of coercion."

With encouragement and design assistance from such a notable right-leaning voice as the Heritage Foundation, Romney felt free to move in this direction to ease the burden of the Commonwealth in covering healthcare costs (emergencies and non-emergencies masquerading as emergencies) that were not paid for by individuals or insurance policies and address some other issues as well, including:

> an expiring federal-government waiver as to how Massachusetts administered its Medicaid program;

> a noticeable drop in number of residents covered by individually purchased policies and rising prices for small group policies;

> the cost of the state's "free care pool" rising each year well beyond intake from the taxes that fed the pool;

> demand from advocacy groups for a long list of non-traditionally covered procedures and goods; and

> employers increasingly dropping health insurance as a benefit.

After much back and forth with the Legislature, the bill passed by 154-2 in the Massachusetts House and unanimously, in the Massachusetts Senate —including the vote of Scott Brown, who won Ted Kennedy's seat in the U.S. Senate in January

2010 by pledging to be the "forty-first vote against ObamaCare." (He did not get the chance because the Democrat-run Senate delayed his swearing in to rush ObamaCare through.)

Romney strongly opposed the employer mandate and wanted an escape to from the individual mandate by allowing people instead to be able to post a bond if they were uninsured and were faced with insurmountable medical bills. When Romney signed the bill, he believed it contained the escape hatch; however, legislators removed the clause just before final passage and Romney carelessly overlooked the final version before he signed it into law in April, 2006.

Thus, Massachusetts residents were the first in the nation to have an individual mandate imposed on them. The Heritage Foundation's healthcare analyst Bob Moffit flew to Boston for the bill signing. Romney vetoed eight sections, but the legislature overrode all. RomneyCare reached deeply in all areas of health insurance and medical services and expanded subsidy coverages. The overwhelmingly Democrat legislature set the threshold for receiving a subsidy so that it included people making just below the median income in the U.S.

To make matters worse, the legislature later destroyed the group-rate, "no frills" private insurance plans allowed under RomneyCare (one that would suit most people) by adding dozens of state mandates, including requiring insurers to cover extras such as chiropractors and *in vitro* fertilization.

The consequence to residents of Massachusetts between passage of RomneyCare and the start of ObamaCare was the highest health insurance premiums in the nation. The requirement on insurers not to refuse new applicants with "pre-existing" conditions, encouraged gaming the system by paying the penalty at tax time and buying insurance only when a major medical need arose.

And RomneyCare did nothing to decrease the extent of third-party involvement in medical payments, further putting off any move towards more market-based direct patient-provider relationships. Of course, any entitlement sold as a way to reduce costs was bound to bring about more state control over prices for medical services and restrictions on availability of more expensive services.

Summing up: The path to ObamaCare

We have seen how a series of poor decisions and bad laws have served to create a less than ideal marketplace for health insurance and a demand push that has accelerated health costs. To summarize:

> The *Wickard v. Filburn* decision that extended the Commerce Clause to give the federal government powers even over *not* engaging in commerce;

> The War Labor Board ruling on fringe benefits in a wage-and-price-control environment that increased the role of third-party payers;

> The McCarran-Ferguson Act that hampered development of a free, nationwide insurance market;

> The Emergency Medical Treatment and Active Labor Act put pressure on hospital finances, increased demand on acute health providers and decreased the sense of need for personal financial responsibility when it comes to certain health services;

103

> Agitation for mandates from "conservatives," — and

> One state's errant leap into individual mandates to dodge the threat of an oppressive national healthcare regulation proposal.

Now let's look at an unfortunate, but perhaps predictable consequence of these developments.

~6~
ObamaCare is Born

According to a September, 2009 USA Today/Gallup poll Americans were broadly satisfied with the quality of their medical care and healthcare costs, but of the two, satisfaction with costs lagged. Overall, 80% were satisfied with the quality of medical care available to them, including 39% who were very satisfied. Sixty-one percent were satisfied with the cost of their medical care, including 20% who are very satisfied. 85% of Americans with health insurance coverage are broadly satisfied with the quality of medical care they receive and with their healthcare costs.

C6-AA http://www.gallup.com/poll/123149/Cost-Is-Foremost-Healthcare-Issue-for-Americans.aspx

But if you want to control people, what better way than to control their bodies? And are not "Liberals" really all about increasing state control? And so they passed ObamaCare.

There are two main issues when it comes to evaluating this law: rights and policy.

Assault on rights and the Constitution

Contra constitutional

As distasteful as the mandate is in RomneyCare, states can enact all sorts of laws without violating the U.S. Constitution. States have been forcing people to do things from the beginning of the republic: drilling for the militia, taking blood tests before marriage, paying for public schools, registering property titles, and making and enforcing vehicle registration and insurance requirements.

But the Tenth Amendment places limits on what Congress can do. (Romney did say that his plan would be a bad idea done federally.) The main difference between the healthcare bills is that RomneyCare is constitutional and ObamaCare is not. Simply put, Congress has no constitutional authority to force citizens to buy a particular product.

Register for the draft at 18 if you are a male? Yes (Article I, section 8). Buy a product? No. Not engaging in commerce by not buying something is not engaging in "commerce among the several States." So the individual's right to decide how to care for his most personal possession, his body, has been diminished considerably, first in Massachusetts, and now in every state.

While the federal penalty for not buying health insurance was reduced to $0 starting in 2019, the structure for it is still part of the law and would as easy to reinstate by a different Congress and president. (Alas, Massachusetts residents cannot escape this burden, as RomneyCare is still on the books.)

Natural rights trammeled

Another assault on natural rights is that religious organizations are now required to provide free sterilization, contraceptives, and abortion-inducing drugs to their employees, even if these services violate their religious beliefs. Thus ObamaCare could conflict with the Clinton-era Religious Freedom Act and, more importantly, the First Amendment. But above all, the law is an affront to traditional American sense of liberty and individualism.

Policy problems

The control regime

Clearly unconstitutional provisions are alone good reasons to terminate this terrible law. As for policy, the law is an ever changing disaster in motion.

> Companies with more than fifty employees have to provide and pay for expensive government-determined health insurance for their employees or face federal fines. Mid-size firms (51-100 workers) are especially stressed. Surely some companies nearing that threshold will elect not to cross it, thus reducing economic growth and employment opportunities.

> The Independent Payment Advisory Board was to have the power to decide which procedures are "worth it" for older individuals through its rationing power over Medicare. If it had not been repealed in the 2018 budget act, Sarah Palin's "death panels" might have materialized. With the cost stress on the system, the IPAB might return.

> Value-based payments, quality reporting requirements, and

government comparative-effectiveness boards will dictate how doctors practice medicine. Eventually, we might see fewer candidates for medical schools. This 2011 paper by the Galen Institute outlines how ObamaCare will be bad for doctors and patients.

> C6-AB http://www.galen.org/topics/the-new-health-law-bad-for-doctors-awful-for-patients/

> And then there are the 159 new boards, agencies, and programs. And supervision of conformity to this law by those kind, unbiased and infallible folks at the Internal Revenue Service.

Executive tweaking

But all the above is just what the law as written outlines. The law itself awards substantial discretion for important decisions to the Secretary of Health and Human Services. There are in fact 3,267 references to "The Secretary" in the Act.

But even this latitude wasn't enough for the Obama regime, which was quite happy to adjust the execution of the law to suit its own purposes—not by asking Congress for amending legislation. The list of changes-by-fiat includes numerous waivers, exemptions, delays, postponements and suspensions. This 2016 Forbes article by Grace Marie Turner summarizes changes up to that date noted by the staff at her Galen Institute:

> C6-AC
> https://www.forbes.com/sites/gracemarieturner/
> 2016/01/26/obamacare-70-changes-make-it-a-
> very-different-law-than-congress-passed/

If ObamaCare is a law, then should not changes be made by the same process? But of course, as Obama averred: "I've got a pen and I've got a phone" so he did as he wished and Congress did not seem to care.

A strong challenge appears

In 2012 a brave and well-argued challenge to ObamaCare, *National Federation of Independent Businesses v. Sebelius* (Kathleen Sebelius, then Secretary of Health and Human Services) was successful in voiding the coerced expansion of Medicaid, but not in voiding the individual mandate.

There was a chance that the Court could have not accepted the case, because of the Anti-Injunction Act —which prohibits judicial review of a suit to prevent a tax before it goes into effect— if the Court viewed the no-insurance penalty as tax. So for the purpose of taking the case, the Court did not view the penalty as a tax. The reasoning of the Roberts-led majority decision on the mandate was a real stretch: it magically turned the mandate into a tax (despite its view that the penalty was not a tax that would kill the suit per the Anti-Injunction Act!). This decision could create further expansion of federal taxing power as well as challenges to ObamaCare, as such "taxes" would not meet the Constitutional requirement for uniformity, as when some states opt out of Medicaid, or their populations differ in participation in ObamaCare. Heretofore, only excise and income taxes were exempt from the apportionment requirement.

Justices Scalia, Kennedy, Thomas, and Alito dissented. They stated that the individual mandate was not a legitimate regulation of interstate commerce, because it compelled people to engage in particular transactions rather than regulating existing transactions, the below is an excerpt from their written dissent:

> "the mere fact that we all consume food and are thus, sooner or later, participants in the 'market' for food, does not empower the Government to say when and what edibles we will buy. That is essentially what this Act seeks to do with respect to the purchase of healthcare."

The dissenters argued that the individual mandate represented an unprecedented abuse of federal power, for the federal government has "never before used the Commerce Clause to compel entry into commerce." Their dissent also argued that the individual mandate was not a legitimate exercise of the power to tax, because the statute described the fine as a "penalty" rather than a tax, and concluded that the Affordable Care act should be overturned in its entirety, as it could not function as intended without the individual mandate.

The majority opinion in some places gives the initial impression that the majority had ruled the Act unconstitutional. Perhaps Roberts had a last-minute change of mind and did a quick rewrite. There was some discussion at the time from court followers as to how the Obama regime might have some damaging information on Roberts.

Perhaps. The Roberts family may have arranged for adoption of two Irish children through a ruse that made the boy and girl seem to come from somewhere in Latin America. Ireland does not permit adoptions by non-residents and does not permit private adoptions, the way the Roberts used. So there could have been a threat of action by the U.S. to assist in a return of the kids to Ireland. The below blog entry by T.J. McCann covers, but does not prove, the circumstances in which Roberts *may* have been vulnerable to blackmail:

110

C6-AD https://libertyborn.word-press.com/2015/03/02/how-roberts-was-black-mailed-to-support-obamacare/

To date, no action has been made to return the Roberts' adopted children back to Ireland.

A second challenge

Other than exemptions for favored groups and administrative delays for the convenience of the government, the most outrageous example of "rewriting" was the Obama IRS deeming that states that did not establish insurance exchanges would qualify for federal subsidies anyway, even though the law was quite specific that they would not.

In March, 2015 the Supreme Court heard oral arguments in *King v. Burwell,* the case challenging the IRS's decision to pay subsidies to lower-income health insurance buyers in states without federal insurance exchanges — even though the ObamaCare legislation authorizes subsidies only in states with exchanges "established by the state." The Obama administration was thus in the self-inflicted position of arguing that the president's signature law says what it doesn't say.

The framers of ObamaCare certainly did not expect thirty-six states to reject the blandishment of federal subsidies and refuse to set up state exchanges. MIT Professor Jonathan Gruber explained why, in a famous videotaped talk back in 2012. "If you're a state and you don't set up an exchange, that means your citizens don't get their tax credits," he said. "If your governor doesn't set up an exchange, you're losing hundreds of millions of dollars of tax credits to be delivered to your citizens." This is the same guru who rejoiced in the stupidity of the American people that allowed the law to pass:

C6-AE
https://www.youtube.com/watch?v=Adrdmmh7bMo

Alas, the *King v. Burwell* challenge failed in the Supreme Court, which in the contorted reasoning of Chief Justice Roberts, ignored the plain text of the law (ten times in the Act) and declared that "state" meant the state as a general term for government, included the federal government. So the subsidies continued. But it was encouraging that there were Governors and legislators who showed an increased willingness to forego federal dollars. Such action showed that a healthy mistrust of centralized command-and-control government was still possible.

Damages

The greatest damage of ObamaCare is the assault on freedom to make decisions about the individual's most important and personal possession: his body. But in addition the act has engendered adverse practical consequences, some planned, others unforeseen.

Impact on medical services

So much for Obama's oft-repeated "If you like your healthcare plan will be able to keep it" and "If you like your doctor you will be able to keep your doctor, period." The unfortunate results of this legislation to many people have been considerable. The numbers change each year, so the below is a general outline of the consequences of ObamaCare.

Less choice in plans

Most existing plans did not meet ObamaCare requirements, so many have been forced to buy now more expensive policies with features they don't want and could never use (maternity coverage for *everybody* including males and post-menopause females) or lower deductibles that they would rather not pay for in higher premiums. And there's no way to opt for a low-cost catastrophic policy. Many younger and generally healthy people have chosen to forego any insurance and deal with the penalty at tax time.

Less choice of providers

The new record keeping and payment systems are forcing doctors in private practice to sell out to hospitals or join "Accountable Care Organizations," thus reducing choices of options for finding a doctor. For families and individuals who prefer to pay for their own healthcare, such care is now less affordable. And smaller hospitals and clinics have felt pressure to merge with larger facilities, a sort of "too big to fail" effect as in the financial realm. There were no fewer than ninety-five hospital mergers in 2014 —the first year ObamaCare was fully in effect— according to Dr. Marty Makary [*Wall Street Journal*, April 20, 2015]. The result is less competition and choice, as discussed in this 2017 Daily Caller article by Matthew Kandrach, president of Consumer Action for a Stronger Economy:

C6-AF http://dailycaller.com/2017/11/21/obamac-are-incentives-are-causing-hospital-monopolies-to-put-profits-over-patients/

Impact on costs of medical services and insurance

Two temporary programs, risk corridors and re-insurance, expired at the start of 2017, so premiums have increased substantially since for persons using them.

Higher health-care costs have arrived. Obama promised premiums would be $2,500 lower by 2013. Of course premiums for the approved plans have meant substantial increases. Mandatory unwanted coverages are a big part of the increases.

Under-enrollment, especially by younger persons, is another. The expectation of ObamaCare's architects that younger, healthier people would opt to start buying health insurance for which they heretofore did not feel the need, or to pay new higher rates than they had paid, was surely a miscalculation that a little common sense could have squelched.

A good analysis of the substantial medical insurance cost increases since the imposition of ObamaCare can be found in this 2017 Forbes article by Robert Book and Paul Howard:

C6-AG
https://www.forbes.com/sites/theapothecary/2017/0
3/22/yes-it-was-the-affordable-care-act-that-in-
creased-premiums/

Impact on state fiscal health

One of ObamaCare's chief initiatives is providing for the expansion of Medicaid. The legislators who wrote this law understood that taxpayer subsidies alone would not be enough to cover the roughly 30 million Americans who did not have health insurance at the time of the law's passage, so they created a provision in ObamaCare that incentivizes states to expand Medicaid programs by offering to pay 100 percent of the cost from 2014 through 2016. The law requires the national government to gradually reduce its share down to 90 percent by 2020. The remaining 10 percent of costs will be covered by the states.

In theory, slowly shifting the expansion burden to the states allows state governments the time necessary to increase tax revenues or make budget cuts to cover the additional expenses. In practice, this works only if the number of people who enroll in Medicaid matches states' expectations. If more people enroll in Medicaid than expected, the burden on the states will be even more costly and could cause significant budgetary and healthcare-related problems.

Unfortunately, a dramatic and unexpected increase in Medicaid enrollments is precisely what has occurred in many of the states that chose to expand. For instance, in Colorado the number of additional people enrolled in Medicaid and the Children's Health Insurance Program (CHIP), which was also receiving significant temporary federal funding boost, grew by 477,000 from 2013 to February 2015, according to the Centers for Medicare and Medicaid Services. That's an increase of 60 percent, well beyond the growth that most state officials initially anticipated.

By 2018, the strain on the budget of adopting states was becoming clear when the new state costs of expanded Medicaid began to set in, as evidenced by stress on education budgets that led to teacher strikes in Kentucky, West Virginia, Arizona and Oklahoma. This 2017 article in Bond Buyer describes the added stress to Maine's finances:

<u>C6-AH</u> https://www.bondbuyer.com/news/maine-medicaid-expansion-vote-adds-stress-to-state-finances

Impact on the federal fisc

The financial impact of ObamaCare hits both subscribers who must pay the expensive exchange policy premiums and the federal treasury, which must pay for the subsidies. In late 2016, a preview of the impact on both the policy payer and the tax payer for the next year is presented in this 2016 Reason Magazine article by Peter Suderman:

<u>C6-AI</u> https://reason.com/blog/2016/12/16/obamacares-subsidies-to-cost-taxpayers-a

As the folks at Reason like to say, there's no such thing as a free lunch!

By 2017 only four of the twenty-three Consumer Operated and Oriented Health-care Cooperatives established under ObamaCare were still operating. Billions in taxpayer loans have been wasted. More on this subject can be found at this American Enterprise Institute site:

<u>C6-AJ</u> https://www.aei.org/publication/another-obamacare-dream-goes-bust/

Negative effects on businesses and their employees

In the first year of ObamaCare, there were many news stories of full-time jobs being converted to part-time to avoid the coverage requirements for employees logging in more than thirty hours a week. This pattern grew as the major provisions took full effect in 2016. A preview was at Staples in early 2015, which shifted many workers to less than full-time. Chris Conover in a 2014 forbes.com blog outlined the problem as it appeared at the time:

C6-AK http://www.forbes.com/sites/chriscon-over/2014/02/24/obamacare-will-cost-2-9-million-or-more-jobs-a-year/

Thus low-income workers are especially affected as their options for coverage are limited to obtaining a Minimum Essential Coverage Plan, purchasing a Bronze plan at a substantial percentage of income, or paying the fines. The real downside of such top-down control is to reduce gross domestic product, the size of the economic pie, and career-type job opportunities. John Goodman of the Goodman Institute describes in this January 2015 article how ObamaCare is hurting the very people it was intended to help:

C6-AL http://www.goodmaninstitute.org/how-obama-care-harms-low-income-workers/

ObamaCare especially harms low-income workers just above the minimum wage level by encouraging employers to reduce hours and remove low-cost mini-med coverage options from remaining full-time workers. This 2014 Forbes article by Bill Cassidy MD, at the time a Congressman from Louisiana and later a U.S. senator, outlines the problem:

C6-AM
https://www.forbes.com/sites/theapothecary/2014/0
9/17/how-obamacares-employer-mandate-harms-
low-wage-workers/

In a report dated January 2017, American Action Forum found that ObamaCare regulations reduced small business pay by at least $19 billion annually. In addition, ObamaCare regulations and rising premiums reduced employment by more than 295,000 jobs nationwide:

> C6-AN
> https://www.americanactionforum.org/research/upd
> ate-obamacares-impact-small-business-wages-
> employment/

Threats to innovation

The United States has long been the leader in developing new pharmaceuticals, medical procedures and medical devices. As examples, below are five innovations or research-in-progress in 2013, the year before ObamaCare took effect, as reported by the American Society of Mechanical Engineers:

>Cutting back on melanoma biopsies with a device from MELA Sciences, (Irvington, New York) that uses missile navigation technologies to optically scan the surface of a suspicious lesion at 10 electromagnetic wavelengths.

> A technology under clinical investigation at Autonomic Technologies, Inc., (Redwood City, California) for blocking sphenopalatine ganglion nerve bundle signals at the first sign of a headache.

>A needle-free diabetes biosensor from Echo Therapeutics (Philadelphia, Pennsylvania) that reads blood analytes through the skin without drawing blood.

>Robotic check-ups using the RP-VITA Remote Presence

Robot produced jointly by iRobot Corp (Bedford, Massachusetts) and InTouch Health (Santa Barbara, California).

>The Sapien transcatheter aortic valve, a life-saving alternative to open-heart surgery for patients who need new a new valve, but can't endure the rigors of the operation, from Edwards Life Sciences (Irvine, California).

This targeted excise tax had adverse effects before its moratorium for 2015 and 2016, including medical technology firms transferring R&D centers and jobs offshore. During 2010-2014 private-equity investment in new U.S. healthcare startups declined, according a January, 2015 article in the *Journal of the American Medical Association*. A 2018 article by the Tax Foundation describes how the predicted negative effects of this tax have occurred to both companies and consumers:

C6-AO https://taxfoundation.org/new-research-provides-more-reasons-to-repeal-the-medical-device-tax/

The tax is still there, in spite of occasional attempts in Congress to end it. It is very possible, but hard to know exactly, that some promising medical devices were never developed because of it.

~7~
Strategy and Solutions

The long-term consequences of ObamaCare could be a federal "single-payer" system, as the private insurers increasingly find it hard to cover claims and for providers and insurers to operate in a business-like way. This outcome could be what Obama and his government-knows-best cohorts had in mind all along.

Barney Frank, the very liberal congressman from Massachusetts, admitted as much in 2009, when asked about single payer by a reporter, as captured in this video:

C7-AA
https://www.youtube.com/watch?v=QLm9t9j-qKM

In April 2016, citing huge losses, United Health Group, the largest healthcare insurance provider, announced it was withdrawing from participation in ObamaCare exchanges.

Around this time other insurers such as Humana, Aetna, and Anthem revealed big losses from ObamaCare subsidized policies. This 2016 Forbes article describes the implications of United Health's withdrawal.

C7-AB
https://www.forbes.com/sites/michaelcannon/2016/
04/19/five-things-aca-supporters-dont-want-you-to-
know-about-unitedhealths-withdrawal-from-obamac-
are

Government as the only healthcare payer could eventually lead to government-run healthcare (single provider). This model has not worked well in the countries where this approach rules. Despite its much heralded presence in Britain's healthcare, the problems of its National Health Service are severe, notorious, and increasingly scandalous in the most fundamental attributes of any healthcare system: access and quality. Waits for care are shocking, as frequently exposed by British media reports (but not much in the U.S.). Access to medical care is so poor in the NHS that the government was compelled to issue England's 2010 "NHS Constitution" in which it was declared that no patient should wait beyond 18 weeks (!) for treatment after a GP referral. And the quality of medical care for cancer, heart disease, and stroke in the NHS and its European equivalents, based on data in the medical journals such as *Lancet Oncology* and *Lancet Neurology* is noticeably deficient compared with survival rates in the U.S. Even blood-pressure treatment has been inferior and less successful than in the U.S. because it more often goes untreated. Ditto for diabetes.

The heinous scandals about the quality of care in NHS hospitals that are repeatedly discovered, investigated, and catalogued with promises of change. These scandals, like the Staffordshire Trust debacle where between 400 and 1,200 neglected and abused patients died in squalid and degrading circumstances, are directly caused by the culture of the NHS, as overtly admitted even by the UK government at its highest levels. Scott Atlas, MD at forbes.com describes the sad state of affairs in a 2013 article:

C7-AC http://www.forbes.com/sites/scottat-las/2013/07/05/happy-birthday-to-great-brit-ains-increasingly-scandalous-national-health-service/

At least there are still private practitioners in the U.K., and one can buy private health insurance. Canada has had a single-payer system since 1984. The long wait times for advanced diagnostic and operations cause many Canadians who have the means to head to the U.S., as described in this 2014 *Forbes* article by senior health economist Bacchus Barua at the Frazer Institute in Canada:

C7-AD http://www.forbes.com/sites/theapothe-cary/2014/06/13/if-universal-health-care-is-the-goal-dont-copy-canada

Back in the states, the 2014 Veterans Administration scandal should serve as a warning to avoid any development that might lead to government someday running healthcare operations, as this CBS News story shows.

C7-AE http://www.cbsnews.com/feature/va-hospi-tals-scandal/

Why not just give veterans with service-related conditions vouchers for care in non-government medical facilities and phase out VA hospitals?

For an overview on the state of ObamaCare exchanges in 2018 visit this Heritage Foundation report by Edmund Haislmaier:

<u>C7-AF</u> https://www.heritage.org/health-care-reform/report/2018-obamacare-health-insurance-exchanges-competition-and-choice-continue

His key points are that at the state level, more insurers exited the Obamacare exchanges in 2018, though not as many as left in either 2016 or 2017. And that more than half (51.3 percent) of all counties have only one insurer offering exchange coverage, and ten states have no exchange competition in any county for 2018.

Solutions

President Trump has made some useful tweaks, but Congress must effect a real repeal. Start immediately with legislation to end all mandates. Trump's repeal of the mandate penalty beginning in 2019 is helpful, but a legislative change would be more assuring.

1) Phase out ObamaCare in a way that will not impact seriously anyone who changed plans to conform to it so that they can make other arrangements over a brief but realistic time. Allow reinstatement of prior or current plans if so desired. Do not allow any new enrollments in ObamaCare exchanges that would entail subsidies.

2) Break the connection between job and health coverage. Disallow deductibility by employers the cost of healthcare insurance for employees. Allow full deductibility in personal income taxes for self-pay healthcare policies. These steps will partially reconnect individuals with the financial realities of healthcare and re-introduce market mechanisms for healthcare services and insurance products. After a few years of increasing

assumption of personal health insurance assumption by individuals, a phase out of the income tax deduction for health insurance could be considered, so there would be no federal government connection with the healthcare sphere, except as needed for military and diplomatic personnel.

3) Modify McCarran-Ferguson to allow a truly free nationwide insurance marketplace. Allow insurance companies to formulate any policies that make actuarial sense and price them in the newly freed market. The likely new availability of high-deductible, catastrophic policies will help restore market forces to the pricing of routine healthcare services, as more of these outlays will be payments from individuals directly to their providers.

4) If the above step is accomplished, establish a federal agency with enforcement powers that will provide support for any policy holder who can present a plausible case that an insurance company did not honor a just claim. This would be a new federal agency, but well worth it for relief from all the entanglements and consequences of ObamaCare and state-regulated medical insurance.

For further reading

Lives at Risk: Single-Payer National Health Insurance Around the World by John C. Goodman, Gerald Musgrave, Devon M. Herrick, and Milton Friedman; 2004, Rowman & Littlefield

Unprecedented: The Constitutional Challenge to Obamacare

by Josh Blackman; 2013, Public Affairs
> C7-AG http://www.unprecedentedcase.com

Surviving the Medical Meltdown: Your Guide to Living Through the Disaster of Obamacare by Lee Hieb, MD; 2015, World News Daily Books
> C7-AH http://superstore.wnd.com/surviving-the-medical-meltdown-e-book/

Overcoming Obamacare: Three Approaches to Reversing the Government Takeover of Health Care by Philip Klein; 2015, Washington Examiner

Restoring Quality Health Care: A Six-Point Plan for Comprehensive Reform at Lower Cost by Scott W. Atlas, MD; 2016, Hoover Institution Press

A weekly newsletter of articles from the Galen Institute is available at
> C7-AI http://ObamacareWatch.org

Afterword

In January 2009 what America needed from its national government was less involvement in everyday life of its citizens, less spending, lower and simpler taxes, less interference with state and local affairs, better border and immigration enforcement and more attention and resources to federal responsibilities to deal with the outside world and any threats from parties not well intended towards us.

What we got in these eight years was much neglect of what was needed and much that was just not only not needed but very negative. In the domestic realm we saw corruption at the Justice Department, spying on citizens, interference with local police, questionable pardons, IRS abuse, damaging interference in secondary and vocational education and student lending; and actions that dampened economic growth, impaired the Internet and flying safety, and a counterproductive setback in the healthcare insurance system.

In the foreign affairs realm we saw deterioration of border control, defense posture, and capabilities in space; and contrary

127

interactions re friends and foes, ransoms for hostages, question-able agreements, and avoidance of dealing with real threats.

In the social realm we saw an assault on common sense and the naturally developed mores of a free people.

A president with un-American ideas, questionable allegiances and inexperience in government at a high level can do a lot of damage. The Obama years remind us that parties need to care-fully vet their presidential candidates. This checklist for parties and voters might be helpful to refer to every four years:

Is the candidate distinguished by accomplishments in government or business?

Who has the candidate's political thinking been influ-enced by?

Is he or she really "of the land" or are there openings for other allegiances?

And voters need to choose according to criteria other than a novel theme, which in this case was the prospect of the first non-white president.

In 2016 voters chose a candidate who promised to undo much of the damage of the Obama regime. If we are lucky, those eight years were just an aberration that will not soon repeat.

34775237R00083

Made in the USA
Middletown, DE
02 February 2019